HEART TO HEART:

Earthy Reflections for Heaven-Bound Believers

By Rev. Wanda McNeill
Editor: Mary Gales Askren

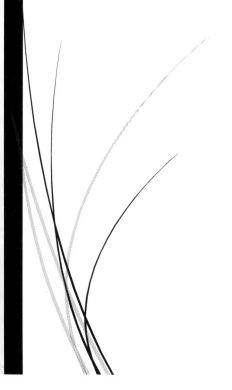

ISBN-10: 1541325753
First Print Publication: Dec. 26, 2016
Cover Photography & Design: Jeffrey F. Morrison
Book Design by: Mary Gales Askren

Printed by CreateSpace, An Amazon.com Company

Dedicated to:

*Those folks throughout the years
who have ears to hear the Gospel
and sense they are in its presence*

CONTENTS

Acknowledgements

INTRODUCTION *3*

ADVENT
      Pondering Heart (Luke 2:19) 7

CHRISTMAS
      Christmas Tonight (Luke 2:1-20) 9

TIME AFTER EPIPHANY
      Baptism Blessing (Matthew 3:13-17) 12
      Why Was I Born? (John 1:29-42) 16

LENT
      Stop Pretending (Matthew 6:1-6, 16-21) 20

HOLY WEEK
      Kingdoms Clash (Luke 22:14-23:56) 23
      Cross – A Place of Paradox (John 19:1-30) 26

EASTER
      Resurrection Hope (Luke 24:1-12) 29
      Peace – Perfect Peace (John 14:23-29) 32

PENTECOST
      Heirs by Adoption (Romans 8:[9-13]14-17) 35

TIME AFTER PENTECOST
      Trust & Obey (Genesis 22:1-14, Matthew 11:29-30). 38
      Politics of Compassion (Luke 7:11-17) 42
      Finding Ourselves In the Ditch (Luke 10:25-37) 47
      Prayer beyond All Prayers (Luke 11:1-13). 50
      Seductive Wealth (Luke 12:13-21). 54
      Fear Not, Little Flock (Luke 12:32-40) 58
      The Good News of Tough Love (Luke 12:49-56). 61

HOLY CROSS DAY
      Cross Action (Mark 8:27-38). 65

ALL SAINTS SUNDAY
      Saintly Sinners (Luke 6:20-31) 69

CHRIST THE KING SUNDAY
      Crucified King (Luke 23:33-43). 74

Notes 78

Wanda McNeill, Biographical Sketch. 85

Acknowledgments

These reflections were not initially intended for publication. They were written to be preached. Therefore, references and citations were not noted. After the decision was made to publish, every effort was made to identify original sources, and when that wasn't possible, to provide information that both acknowledged the contribution of other minds and provided the diligent reader with avenues for further exploration. If there are omissions, they are entirely unintentional; both the author and the editor wish to give credit where credit is due. Both understand that others influence our ideas, and are grateful to those individuals whose works contributed to the development of the ideas explored in these reflections. However, it must also be noted that some of the examples are widely used in spiritual writing, and therefore, it was not possible to identify an original source.

Gratitude must be expressed to Arla Hamman Poindexter, who diligently proofed each sermon after it was edited to increase the likelihood that this publication would be free of errors. Jeffrey F. Morrison must also be thanked for his cover design, which captured both the beauty and spirit of these reflections.

INTRODUCTION

Nothing good is ever lost; it becomes part of our character.

I wish I could take credit for that idea, but I can't. I heard it while listening to an audiobook, *The Shell Seekers* by Rosamunde Pilcher[1], and was struck by the plain truth it expressed. And yet, I can think of no better statement with which to begin this introduction, because the goodness of the friendship I shared with the author of these reflections, Pastor Wanda McNeill, has helped to shape my character.

We arrived in a small, agricultural community from different directions, not only geographically, but also professionally and emotionally. Wanda had stepped down from her position as associate pastor of the Lutheran Church of the Reformation in Washington, DC, where she had also been one of the founders of the Southeast Ministry, a ministry of which she spoke often. Her involvement began when she attended a community meeting, and continued for nearly two decades, as she partnered with others to build an inner-city ministry which continues to bring hope to ex-offenders and welfare mothers through programs – such as a job readiness program – that help to transform their lives.

The *Congressional Record* (Vol. 153, No. 115) makes note of what she accomplished with a tribute presented to the U.S. House of Representatives on July 17, 2007. A "whereas" litany outlines the key movements of her life, but the introduction provides a succinct summary of her work: "Pastor McNeill, on the surface, was not an obvious candidate to take on such work in an inner-city neighborhood, having been born and raised in Sioux City, Iowa. But Pastor McNeill has touched the lives of thousands in Washington, DC, and this city will be forever grateful for her dedication to those in need."

At the same time, I was climbing out of the pit of depression. After building a successful career as a journalist in the state's capitol, I set that aside to help a floundering nonprofit. Having served on the board of directors for nearly a year, I had seen the organization go through three executive directors and suspected there were issues about which the board knew nothing. I was right, but in addressing the issues, which ranged from mismanagement of grant funding to improper supervision of volunteers, I stepped on toes and was eventually asked to resign the position I held.

Finding another position proved to be difficult, primarily because the experience had shattered my self-confidence. At the same time that I was experiencing this professional crisis, I was dealing with the chaos of my dad's last days. Our family had been profoundly broken when my mother died 30 years earlier, and the decisions which faced me and my brothers only magnified that break. I fought hard against acknowledging the toll all of this was taking, but was forced to admit the truth when I caught myself pointing a finger at my head, as though it were a gun, and making a sound in my throat that mimicked a gun shot. Eventually, I accepted a position with a small weekly newspaper, rented a sunlit house in the community, and began the arduous task of climbing out of that pit.

Wanda's hand guided me. We arrived within weeks of each other, and I was assigned to write a story about her as an introduction to the primarily Lutheran community. I can still remember sitting in her office – it was the only time we met there – and feeling hope stir within me. I was Catholic and knew I would not be attending services at the Lutheran church, but I wanted to know this woman better. At the end of the interview, I hesitantly asked if we could get together for lunch sometime, and she most graciously agreed.

We met at the local café – the new Lutheran pastor and the new Catholic reporter – and talked about demons. It is my practice to meditate on a passage of Scripture each morning, and that morning I had reflected on one of the passages in which Jesus drives out demons. With the demon of depression tearing me apart, I desperately longed for healing, and so the passage had resonated with me. I wanted to know, though, the lived experience of those possessed by demons in Scripture. I don't think Wanda expected a theological discussion over the homey food the café offered. That was probably the only time she didn't expect to find herself engaged in a theological discussion with me.

In the years which followed, we would have dinner together on Friday evenings when our schedules permitted, which wasn't often. As the lone reporter for our community, I covered everything from city council meetings to sports events, and Fridays often found me at games – football, basketball, volleyball, whatever was in season. However, I came to cherish those dinners. She would have a glass of white wine, I would have a Sam Addams and we would grapple with something – a new insight I'd had during prayer, a new idea she'd encountered while studying. Those hours were a balm to my spirit, not only in the early months, when I was struggling with depression, but also later, when I found myself engaged in a guerilla war I never understood with another member of the staff. To that craziness, Wanda's presence brought peace. To the isolation I felt in what I came to realize was an insular community, Wanda brought companionship. To a soul thirsty for spiritual sustenance, Wanda brought deep, satisfying conversation.

On occasion, I did have the opportunity to hear her preach – the community Christmas Eve worship service, ecumenical worship services in the park on summer evenings, at a funeral when a colleague's wife died. Each time, I was struck by the way she presented big ideas in a way that was easy to understand and by the poetic way she used language. Earlier this year, when I learned she was entering hospice as the result of a terminal lung disease, I audaciously asked if I could have her sermons to edit into a book. It was a selfish request; I wanted to hold not only in memory, but in my hands, a tangible reminder of her beautiful heart, her great understanding, and her radiant faith.

However, this wonderful woman, who had served as interim pastor for another small church after receiving her diagnosis, surprised me. Having been forced by her condition to stop preaching, she felt the need for another project, and culled from the files which held the sermons from her ministry which lasted nearly 30 years, those included in this book. I cried when I read her Christmas sermon because I'd heard her preach it. I didn't know then how much friendship could bring forth in our lives a Christmas miracle, the miracle of God's presence in conversation and human kindness.

May these reflections bless you as much as Wanda's friendship has blessed me.

Mary Gales Askren
The First Sunday of Advent, 2016

ADVENT

PONDERING HEART

'But Mary treasured all these things
and pondered them in her heart' – Luke 2:19

Advent and Christmas are the seasons meant for pondering, for considering what God is doing and has done for us. It is the season to take to heart our intimate relationship with God and to intentionally nurture that relationship. Perhaps, pondering is a feminine thing – men might be more prone to question, analyze, or evaluate. Pondering has a quality about it that is more than mere thinking about something. The Greek tell us the word means to 'put things together.' So Mary must have reflected on all the parts of her life – her visit from Gabriel and what that meant for her future, her feelings of uncertainty, her personal history of living the simple life of a humble Jewish girl, her unswerving obedience to God, and how things would all change as God's plan for her unfolded. She was putting all those things together and waiting ... waiting on the Lord's will to be revealed.

Pondering is drifting with the Spirit in a way that gives God opportunity to join us and nudge us toward God's divine will and purpose. Pondering opens our hearts and minds to God's unexpected ways. Mary had a great deal to ponder. However, we are no different; we too have much to ponder.

The author, Sue Monk Kidd[1], tells of visiting a monastery once before Christmas. She was taking a walk on the grounds when she passed a monk who was also taking a walk. She greeted him with *'Merry Christmas.'* The monk's response caught her off guard. *'May Christ be born in you,'* he replied. Those words carry a great impact. Advent is a time of spiritual preparation and transformation. It is 'discovering God wants us to allow Christ to be born in our waiting hearts.'

Have you ever thought about the inn keeper in the nativity story who refused a room to Mary and Joseph? I have thought of the inn keeper and fussed at him in my mind. I would have found some small room for Mary and Joseph, or given up my own bedroom. After all, here was a travel-weary couple in need, with a young woman due to deliver her firstborn at any minute. Well, now is our chance to welcome Jesus who is still looking for room in our hearts.

A great mystic of the past, Meister Eckhart[2], once said, *'What good is it to me if Mary gave birth to the Son of God hundreds of years ago, if I do not give birth to the Son of God in my time and my culture. We are all meant to be Mothers of God, for God is always needing to be born.'*

Ponder on that long and hard. Is your heart manger-shaped and ready to receive the baby Jesus? Before you say, 'Not me, I could not be the Mother of the baby Jesus,' recall where God places his treasure on this earth. God's treasure is not gold, but gospel; not silver, but good news; not hard cold cash but grace, love, and peace. God could have left his treasure with politicians, those responsible for collecting taxes, building schools, and passing laws, but God didn't. God could have left his treasure with the high priests, but he didn't. God left his treasure in the least likely of places - in the love, care, and nurture of a first-century peasant woman chosen as the 'handmaiden of the Lord.' God's treasure was left with the most powerless figure in the ancient world.

Look at us, we are not powerful and important in the eyes of the world. Are we willing to be 'handmaidens' of the Lord in the 21st century? Jesus still needs a home, a place to be loved and served. Are we willing for Christ to be born anew in us? Ponder on that long and hard.

Advent/Christmas Devotion for Women of the ELCA
Date Unknown

HEART TO HEART

CHRISTMAS

CHRISTMAS TONIGHT!

Everywhere, everywhere, Christmas tonight!
Christmas in lands of fir-tree and pine,
Christmas in lands of palm-tree and vine,
Christmas where snow peaks stand solemn and white,
Christmas where cornfields stand sunny and bright,
Christmas where children are hopeful and gay,
Christmas where old men are patient and gray,
Christmas where peace, like a dove in its flight,
Broods o'er brave men in the thick of the fight;
Everywhere, everywhere, Christmas tonight!
For the Christ-child who comes is the Master of all;
No palace too great, no cottage too small. [1]

The poetry of Phillips Brooks says it all – everywhere it is Christmas tonight. It is the old, old story that we have come to hear tonight. It is an ancient story, a primal story. Yet, we have all come even though we know the story – a babe is born, angels sing, shepherds gather. Still, we strain to see the crèche and to be comforted by the familiar words of Scripture as we sing the Christmas carols we love. The ancient story we gather to hear again has a hauntingly strange power over us, making us forever young and forever hopeful.

Tonight, we celebrate the moment when the veil between heaven and earth separates, and God in all God's divinity chooses to take on our human dust. Imagine that – dust and divinity mix and mingle and become one in the Christ child – the Christ child, who grew up to be Christ on the cross. Tonight is the fulfillment of the promised moment when God would send a Messiah to save us from our sins, to teach us how to live, to be God in our midst. Never again would we wonder what God was like because Jesus is God wearing our flesh and our blood, our skin and our bones.

Tonight, we celebrate the Incarnation. The Incarnation is the incredible mystery in which our God takes on human flesh in order to be one with us. God in Jesus comes to dance on our dance floors, to cry at our funerals, to eat our bread, and drink our wine. When God sent his son, God sent part of his very heart, so he comes not as a human disguised as God or as God disguised as a human, but as one made of the same stuff we are made of, and one made of the same stuff that God is made of. Therefore, God could be for us Emmanuel – God with us.

There once was a little girl who had trouble going to sleep at night. After she was tucked into bed and had said her prayers, she would call to her mother to bring her a drink of water, and then to check under bed for things that go bump in the night, and then to adjust her night light, and on and on it would go. Her mother reassured her, *'God is with you.'* *'I know,'* she would reply, *'I just wish God had skin on.'* Jesus comes to us as God with skin on to be for us the love of God in person, to teach us how to love and how to live and how to die.

There is something profoundly special about this holy night. It is special in our personal histories as well as in our communal histories. We can probably remember with ease the Christmas Eves of our childhood, when we went to Grandma's house, or were in the Christmas pageant, or enjoyed family gatherings. A greeting card may say it best: *'Backward, turn backward, O time in your flight; make me a child again, just for tonight.'* Oh, how wonderful it would be to have a child-like heart again on Christmas Eve so the stars would be brighter and the air crisper, and you could almost hear the flutter of angels' wings. With child-like hearts, maybe we would be more receptive to the message of Christmas.

The message of Christmas is love.

The love of God brought this world into being. Love hung a billion galaxies in the sky, and maneuvered the mountains and opened up oceans. But God wanted more, God wanted all the people on earth whom he loved to love him as he loved them. God had tried to get the message across in the Scriptures, and through the children of Israel, and with the prophets. Still, people did not get the message, so God tried one more thing – God sent his own son to deliver the message of love.

I hope tonight, this holy night, you can forget the presents waiting for you under the tree, or the eggnog and cookies, or the cards that didn't get sent. Let your child-like heart join in the manger scene, rub shoulders with the shepherds, feel the warmth of the animals' breath, and hear the baby's cry. The nativity is not history, rather it continues every time you open your heart and welcome Jesus. *'For unto you is born this day a savior who is Christ the Lord.'* A Savior who is always on your side – defending you, forgiving you, listening to you, loving you. What a gift God gave us when he stepped out of his divinity in heaven and into the dust of this earth!

The Grinch from Dr. Seuss has the right idea:

And the Grinch with his grinch-feet ice-cold in the snow
stood puzzling and puzzling, 'How can it be so?'
It came without ribbons! It came without tags!
And he puzzled three hours, till his puzzler was sore,
then the Grinch thought of something he hadn't before!!!
Maybe Christmas, he thought, doesn't come from the store
Maybe Christmas, perhaps... means a whole lot more. [2]

The Grinch got this one right. Christmas means much, much more. Christmas means God loves us, each and every one and wants to be with us. Christmas means Emmanuel – God is with us.

AMEN.

Scripture: Luke 2:1-20
Community Christmas Eve Service, 2008
Lake Preston, S.D.

TIME AFTER EPIPHANY

BAPTISMAL BLESSINGS

I am a baptism enthusiast. I think baptism is one of the greatest gifts God has given us. Of course, the greatest gift of all is Jesus. I would rather baptize than anything else I can think of doing. So, the Festival of the Baptism of our Lord is my kind of day, and it brings with it a flood of fond memories.

On Baptism of our Lord Sunday in 1989, I baptized thirteen (13) children from two- to twelve-years-old. I was serving a congregation that met in a fire hall at Bowie, Maryland. As I worked with the Sunday school and Vacation Bible School, I discovered kids who, for one reason or another, hadn't been baptized. At that worship service, there was a lot of confusion, excitement, and joy as families and friends crowded into the fire hall for the celebration. I had trouble sleeping for a week before the baptisms because I was so excited. I kept thinking: What possibilities could God have in mind for those beautiful children? What lies ahead of them on their journey of faith?

I daresay that same kind of question might have crossed John's mind, too, as Jesus came forward to be baptized. John hesitated, but Jesus was insistent. *'Let it be so now.'* It became readily apparent that who baptized whom was not a matter of power or seniority, but rather an issue of *'fulfilling all righteousness,'* or doing God's will. Countless books have been written, and arguments made, about why Jesus, sinless Son of God would want to be baptized. My own theory is that Jesus would do whatever was necessary to be one with us. When we are baptized we take on Jesus' baptism, and we are bound to him in his life, death, and resurrection. Therefore, his baptism becomes our baptism – his blessing becomes our blessing. *'This is my Son, the Beloved, with whom I am well pleased.'* What a moment! What a blessing!

The amazing part was that Jesus' blessing was not earned. He hadn't done anything yet. Jesus was being blessed simply for being alive. It was a blessing that went to the core of Jesus' being – from the heart of God; they had a profoundly deep relationship. This was a covenant relationship between God, the giver, and Jesus, the receiver. In our baptism too, God is the giver and we the receivers.

Baptism is called a Sacrament of Destination, because baptism is not simply a one-time event. Rather, baptism is a continuous process as our faith journey unfolds. God does everything God can do to bring to blossom the seeds of faith and potential that are planted deep in our souls. So today when we speak of Jesus' baptism we are speaking of our own.

Matthew's gospel makes it clear that three things happen at our baptism: the Spirit of God is given; we are claimed as a Child of God and called Beloved; and we are blessed. Our baptisms are not as dramatic as Jesus' baptism, but they are just as profound. At our baptism, when we receive the Holy Spirit, we also receive a new identity. *'Child of God, you have been marked by the Holy Spirit and sealed by the cross of Christ forever.'*[1] Our new name, Child of God, is terribly important. Child of God is our deep-down identity, not the kind of label we wear on the outside. The labels of the world call us Mom or Dad, student, employee, or one of an endless array of other labels that can come and go, be taken from us or outgrown. But, Child of God speaks to the core of our being, and to the heart of who we are and whose we are. We are a Beloved child, precious in God's sight.

When I do baptism preparation, I tell parents the most important thing they will do for their son or their daughter is to teach that child how much God loves them, that their child is a Child of God. Why does that matter? We live in a world full of voices that whisper, shout, or insinuate negative or positive things at us. The voices say, 'you are too young or too old, too fat or too skinny, a failure or a success;' they say, 'you do or don't count.' The world is organized in a competitive fashion where we work and play, buy and sell; there are winners and there are losers – that is life.

The trouble is this: The voices of the world can be so persistent, they start renting space in our heads and we believe them, and respond to them, by beating up on ourselves saying, 'I am not good enough' or 'I am not worthy.' We listen to the outside voices rather than the small inner voice of God that says, 'It is not what you do or how you look that is important; rather it is *who* you are at the core of your being, which is Child of God, that matters.' When we have our core identity right, it affects our self-esteem and happiness. When we know the bedrock of who we are is located in our being a Child of God, then no whispers, no gossip, no negative judgment or commendations, not even applause and accolades, can mess us up.

It isn't easy to grasp how much God loves us, and it may take a lifetime to come to the realization that God, the Source of our being, brought each of us into existence with a uniqueness all our own that pleases God. The fact that we are God's beloved can remain a lofty idea unless we claim our baptismal promises and live into them. It is kind of like winning the lottery; that's great, but if you don't turn in the ticket and claim your prize it doesn't matter. It is only when you claim the prize that things can happen.

God knew that in our sinful state we would have trouble getting our heads and hearts around the idea of God's immense love for us, so God decided to share his very Spirit with us. Life is not easy; there are trials and temptations, but God's Spirit is available, if we take God seriously and ask for the Holy Spirit to help us meet and master life's challenges. When God shares his own Spirit with us, we are given power beyond our imagining.

There is a popular story about a buzzard, a bat, and a bumble bee that explains what I am trying to say. Put a buzzard in a six- by eight-foot pen that is open at the top and the buzzard is a prisoner; it needs a runway of about ten to twelve feet to get airborne. Without a runway, the buzzard is a total prisoner and he won't try to fly. The bat is a nimble dive-bombing creature, who in the same pen with the open top, won't escape. He will only shuffle around helplessly on the floor. The bat needs elevation, or a shelf to throw himself over, in order to fly. Then, there is the bumble bee; put him in an open tumbler and he will be there until he dies. He will try desperately to work his way out of the sides or the bottom, but he never sees an escape route at the top.

We are all a bit like the buzzard, the bat, and the bumble bee. We keep our heads down, our noses to the grind stone, trying the same old ways and forgetting to look up, forgetting to see the heavens open and the powerful Spirit of God descend on us, bringing countless possibilities. When life becomes a burden, pressing us down, stressing us out and overwhelming us, we forget to look up and see the Spirit. We forget to listen-up and hear the words, 'You are my Beloved.'

Children of God, we have been given the priceless gift of the Holy Spirit in our baptism – claim it and live into it.

AMEN.

Scripture: Matthew 3:13-17
January 13, 2008
Lake Preston/North Preston Lutheran Church, Lake Preston, S.D.

WHY WAS I BORN?

Have you seen the mind/body issue of the *Time Magazine* issue from January 17, 2005? It is entitled, *'The Science of Happiness.'*[1] It has some interesting articles such as: 'Is joy in your genes?' 'Does God want you happy?' 'Why we need to laugh.' The issue is titled, 'The Science of Happiness,' but happiness is too limiting a word. It also addresses life satisfaction, fulfillment, purpose, meaning, and engagement in life.

The publication raises some interesting questions, such as: What are the major contributors to life satisfaction? Are married people happier than single people? I will let you in on the answer to that one – married people aren't necessarily happier than single people, unless they were happier before they married. Is money a contributor to happiness? Well, yes, but only to a certain point – where basic needs are met, not beyond.

Of course, statistics report religion plays a role in life satisfaction. Sixty-two percent (62%) of those surveyed credited spiritual life and worship with contributing to their happiness. Seventy-five percent (75%) said contributing to the lives of others was a source of satisfaction. The main reason religion played such a significant role is that it gives people a sense of connectedness: We know from whence we came and to whence we go, and have a purpose while we are here. We not only have a belief in God, but also a sense of community.

This study of life satisfaction fits with the Epiphany season, and this gospel, because one of the themes of Epiphany is 'Call.' Baptism is our primary call from God and becomes the springboard to answer basic life questions such as: *Why was I born? What do I do with my life now that I am here?* Baptism is where God puts God's claim on us*: I have called you by name and you are mine.*

John's Gospel asks questions to which we all want answers. John the Baptist had a group of disciples following him, but the time had come for John to throw his backing to Jesus. His disciples must decide where their loyalties will go. When Jesus approaches John, John gives Jesus an introduction to end all introductions: *'Here is the Lamb of God who takes away the sin of the world. The Lamb who saves us from our sin ... baptizes with the Spirit. This is the Son of God.'* The next day, John and his disciples were standing around and Jesus walks by, and John again exclaims *'Look, here is the Lamb of God.'*

The phrase, 'Lamb of God' was not new to the disciples. Images of lambs as temple sacrifice were common as was the image of the suffering servant. Just using the term 'Lamb of God' would speak volumes about what lay ahead for Jesus. Throughout Scripture, lambs are associated with gentleness, innocence, dependence, and vulnerability. We have become accustomed to the idea of Jesus as Lamb, who takes away sin. That image reveals the surprisingly gentle way that God deals with our sin. You would think sin deserves rebuke, judgment, and punishment; yet in the face of sin, we get a defenseless, innocent lamb, an animal that has no claws, no sharp teeth, can't move fast, and when attacked, can only accept the blows and inevitable fate. If John had announced Jesus as 'Lion of God to track down sinners,' it would have made more sense. 'Lamb of God' says something very profound about the way God saves us through Jesus Christ, about the way Jesus served, and about the way we are to serve others.

Jesus walks by; two disciples follow him. Jesus turns and asks, *'What are you looking for?'* The writer of the Gospel of John was terribly gifted. He wrote on two levels at the same time. The question is addressed to the disciples – right beside Jesus, *'What are you looking for?'* The question is also addressed to you – right here, right now, *'What are you looking for?'*

The disciples' response to Jesus is based on who the disciples recognize Jesus to be. Our response is also based on who we recognize Jesus to be. The disciples wanted to know Jesus better and responded to his question, 'What are you looking for?' with *'Where are you staying?'* That's an interesting response; you might have expected something different. After all, they could have asked practically any question since they were speaking to the Lamb of God. They could have asked questions like, 'What is the meaning of life? Or, why is there suffering in the world? Instead, they asked about his housing arrangement.

This seems strange, but maybe it isn't. These disciples didn't want abstract concepts or theoretical speculations; rather, they wanted to know Jesus, and to be with him, and to follow him. It was only by doing what he did that they could become his disciples. It is only by doing as Jesus did that we become disciples. When we act as he commands, we live into his life – his life and ours become intertwined. Jesus responds, "Come and see," which is the equivalent of 'Follow me.' It is a call to discipleship – the call not just to know who Jesus is, but to do as Jesus did. The call to discipleship is an invitation to purposeful living.

The search for purpose – 'Why was I born? – is an age-old one, and one that has produced anxiety down through the ages. Growing up on a farm in Iowa, I can remember sitting in the barn yard, watching the animals and wondering, why am I a person and not a cow? What does a person do that an animal doesn't do? Several times during my childhood, I recall going to my pastor with my concerns – concerns that caused me agony then, and must have been pretty intense for me to recall them so clearly years later. I recall being brushed off by the pastor and told not to worry. I remember him saying, 'It doesn't matter.' It mattered then and it matters now.

Theologian Paul Tillich[2] says, 'our age-old anxiety is the result of our being finite in the face of finitude and the threat of nothingness.' This might parallel the modern-day heightened awareness in spirituality, which could be interpreted as a quest for meaning and purpose in the face of the finite, of non-being and death. Haven't we all lost loved ones and worried for fear they will be forgotten? Haven't we all heard laments or said them ourselves? There must be

HEART TO HEART

more to life than this rat race! Why is it I have everything I've wanted and still feel so empty? Is this all there is to life?

God's claim on us at our baptism is the beginning point to finding meaning and purpose in our lives. It is our choice, nudged by the Spirit, to respond to God's initiative to 'come and see,' and to live into our baptism, developing the gifts God has given us. The question of life and meaningful purpose are on-going throughout the various stages of life; it is never completely answered. It is a continuous search. Likewise, discipleship is not a one-time thing: I am a disciple. Discipleship is a daily transformation by the power of the Spirit, an on-going process as we daily learn how to love more deeply – love God, love ourselves, and love others.

This *Time Magazine* issue is about us and our happiness. Discipleship is about others, but the two are closely related. When we recall the life of Martin Luther King, Jr., we call the life of a man who knew his identity as a child of God. He sensed his call to use his gifts so strongly that death was not a threat. He chose the 'weapon of love,' the same weapon that the Lamb of God used, to change the face of American society. Listen to this quote: *'We will counter your force of violence with soul force. We will match your ability to hate with our ability to love.'*[3]

Martin Luther King had to do what he did. He had to do what he did, which was to live into his call. Each of us is called to do the same. The world only needed one Martin Luther King to change the face of American society the way he did, but the world needs many Martin Luther Kings to face the injustices in the world. We are called to act in love, according to our giftedness, in a world filled with injustice, and in so doing we help ourselves as we help others.[4] There is much justice work to do.

What are you looking for? Discipleship in Jesus Christ offers each of us a life filled with meaning, purpose, satisfaction, and the Spirit! You need only come and see. Come and see.

AMEN.

Scripture: John 1:29-42
January 16, 2005
Lutheran Church of the Reformation, Washington, D.C.

LENT

STOP PRETENDING:
ASH WEDNESDAY MEDITATION

In my life before I was a pastor, I was a Mom and attended football games. A young man who lived with us was a quarterback, so I went to cheer him on and learned to yell and scream with the best of the parents. As a spectator at one game, I found myself sitting next to Justin, a preschooler. We engaged in the usual pre-school chatter. I asked Justin how old he was; he held up four stubby fingers. A little while later, I felt a tug on my sleeve; Justin motioned for me to bend down to his level, so he could tell me something. Justin whispered, *'Do you know the word pretend?'* *'Yes,'* I nodded. *'Well,'* Justin responded, *'sometimes I pretend I am this many.'* He held up six fingers. Do we know the word, 'pretend'? Yes, Justin, even adults know the word, 'pretend'; pretending is not a childhood phenomenon.

Of course, adults call it by other names, such as 'making a good impression' or 'putting your best foot forward.' We do and say things that exemplify those characteristics valued in our society, such as happiness or successfulness. Presenting ourselves in a good light is fine, but taken to extremes, it can become pretentious, phony, or arrogant. The Gospel has a word for it – hypocrite – because we end up being something or someone we are not, primarily for the sake of impressing others and ourselves. When we act or think in ways that give a false impression, then we are pretending, and that is hypocrisy.

Generally, we are pretty good people, better than most. Our sins are small and insignificant, not big sins like murder or adultery. However, on Ash Wednesday we are called to set aside hypocrisy, and to do an honest examination of our hearts, to see ourselves as we truly are, with sins of omission and commission, sins that are individual and corporate. We also need to acknowledge the sins hidden deep on the back side of our hearts, such as negative thoughts, fantasies, racism, judgmental attitudes, or greed; all of that needs to come to light. Do you know what I mean? While we are fooling others about how good we are, we may have fooled ourselves and glossed over our own failings. In fact, we may have gone so far as to accept the majority of our sins as normal behavior and become comfortable with them.

However, when Ash Wednesday comes along, we are confronted with the deep truth that we share in the fallen nature of the human race that makes us sinful from our mother's womb. As part of a broken world, we also carry wounds of brokenness from our childhood or from exposure to the world. These wounds are so deep within the recesses of our souls, or suppressed in our minds, that we might not even be aware of them, but they are all known to God. Because we are wounded, we also need to beware of beating ourselves up too much – what is, is! We are not all bad, even though we are sinful; there is a basic goodness in all of us, despite our fallen nature. We are sinners, yes. But, we are a mixed bag of good and not-so-good, of honesty and hypocrisy.

As sinners on this Ash Wednesday, we need to be painfully aware of the sinful nature that results in our mortality. But, more than that, we need to be aware of the fact that God loves us despite our sinfulness. What does God desire of us? Psalm 51 tells us that God desires truth in our inward being: *'The sacrifice acceptable to God is a broken spirit; a broken and contrite heart, Oh God, thou will not despise.'*[1] God desires a spirit fully in touch with the reality of our fallen humanity and sorry for it. We may not understand our condition, or why we do what we do, but God understands us and loves us still. So, our Lenten demeanor, although penitent, is also full of confidence and hope.

Today we have an opportunity to receive ashes on our foreheads. The ashes are a reminder of our origins, when God breathed life into the dust of the earth and we came into being. Then, in baptism, God put his claim on us and we received the mark of the cross on our foreheads. Baptism is God returning us to our created nature and the promise of life eternal with God. The cross of ash signifies both, where we came from and where we are going - our origin and our destiny.

Ash Wednesday marks the beginning of our 40-day Lenten journey. Lent is a time when we turn to God who has already turned to us. *God is gracious and merciful, slow to anger, and abounding in steadfast love.*[2] God is our Source and our Salvation, who wants to be with us always. The shadow of the cross is in the distance and the glimmer of the empty tomb is beyond. Today, we confess our sins, *Sinner that I am,* and receive forgiveness, *Savior that I have.* God's love is greater than all our sins, and God's love is everlasting.

AMEN

Scripture: Matthew 6:1-6, 16-21
February 10, 2016
Bethlehem Lutheran Church, Rockford, Ill.

HOLY WEEK

KINGDOMS CLASH:
PALM SUNDAY & PASSION MEDITATION

During Holy Week, two different kingdoms clash. There was the kingdom of the world, steeped in power and violence, and the kingdom of God, filled with peace and goodwill.

Jesus rode into Jerusalem on streets lined with palm branches to the cheers of people shouting, *'Hosanna to the Son of David.'* Jesus was known as a Hebrew holy man, hailed by peasants, lepers and others who experienced his miracles and healings firsthand. On Palm Sunday, Jesus' appearance said it all: He was riding a donkey, holding an olive branch – symbols that shouted peace. The way he rode demonstrated the submissive authority he would show all week. For those familiar with scriptures, his actions claimed the messiahship that his mouth never uttered. Everything about Jesus personified the Kingdom of God.

On the other side of Jerusalem, there was a parade, too, coming from Rome. It was a garrison of soldiers on stately white horses -- you could hear the clatter of the horses' hooves against the cobblestone, hear the creak of their leather saddles, see their swords swinging at their sides. These were solders in battle dress; they were impressive; they looked ready for action – and they were. They had come to keep peace during Passover; their mere presence controlled the crowds. Everything about them shouted power and the kingdom of the world.

Do you get the picture? From the east came peaceful Jesus on his donkey, and from the west came the powerful garrison of soldiers on horseback. They both blended into the scene of political and religious pandemonium that was the Passover. Jerusalem took on a carnival-like atmosphere as thousands of pilgrims crowded the streets. There were baying camels, the aroma of roasting lamb in the air, food vendors hawking their wares, and pilgrims chanting prayers. Roman soldiers kept watch for fear this chaos might erupt at any moment.

The week moved quickly after Jesus' entry into Jerusalem. On Thursday night, after supper, Jesus and his disciples went to the Garden of Gethsemane for Jesus to pray. Jesus had finished his prayers of submission to God's will when Judas and some soldiers arrived. Judas greeted Jesus with a kiss – a kiss of betrayal. From that moment, all was done in the dark of night and in the pre-dawn hours, out of sight, so Jesus' followers wouldn't know and cause a problem.

Jesus had two trials. The first was the Jewish trial with the Sanhedrin, which was comparable to the Supreme Court. They met to formulate a charge against Jesus that would be sufficient to merit the Roman death penalty of crucifixion, because Jews didn't crucify. The High Priests used what Jesus said about the temple being destroyed and rebuilt again in three days; they called it blasphemy. The penalty for blasphemy was death. Then, the second trial was with Pilate, who was the Roman governor; only he could order the crucifixion. Although Pilate was reluctant to give the order, he did. And so, Jesus of Nazareth was crucified.

In the passion narrative, it seems that everything Jesus' opponents attempted was successful. They got the ruling they wanted: to crucify this radical rabbi who was challenging the religious establishment. Everything for which Jesus stood was defeated. A friend became a betrayer; a leader of disciples denied his master; and religious leaders accused a holy man of being irreligious. An innocent man, Jesus of Nazareth, was declared guilty, tortured and executed while a criminal went free.

There is no place where the kingdom of earth and the Kingdom of God clash more than on the cross. There, on the cross, was one final reversal that no one saw coming. When Pilate declared the verdict of death for Jesus of Nazareth, everyone knew the cross was inevitable. They were little aware of the transforming power of the cross that took evil and turned it into good, took death and turned it into life. The cross was not the end of the story. For the apparent defeat of one man, Jesus, opened the Kingdom of God to the entire world.

Easter morning tells the rest of the story.

AMEN.

Scripture: Luke 22:14-23:56
Palm/Passion Sunday, April 20, 2016
Bethlehem Lutheran Church, Rockford, Ill.

CROSS: A PLACE OF PARADOX

Life and death collide on the cross. For all intents and purposes, on Good Friday, it appears that death is the victor. By the time Jesus' body was nailed to the cross, he had been beaten and flogged, and a crown of thorns had been pressed into his skull so that blood ran down his face. He was suffering constant, agonizing pain from the nails; in the heat of the day, flies and gnats would have been buzzing around his head and face, annoying him; and the more blood he lost, the thirstier he became.

Thankfully, Jesus died after six hours; a quick death was considered merciful. Some who were crucified lived for days, and had a slow agonizing death. The physical pain is easy to imagine, but the emotional pain and the spiritual pain would have been excruciating. The goal of death by crucifixion was not simply the death of a victim, but intimidation, shame, and humiliation as the victim became a public spectacle. It must have been especially painful for Jesus, because he knew he had fulfilled his mission to embody the love of God in the world. Perhaps that was too much love for the world to bear, because by his actions he stood in silent judgment of others. Deep down, the world knew the truth – that love is powerful – and they could not tolerate that truth.

What men intended for evil, God used for good. Have you ever considered this: What if Jesus had not died on the cross? What if Jesus had been kicked by a camel and died of those injuries? What if Jesus had died an old man in his sleep? If those things had happened, we would never have known the depth of God's love. Jesus' death on the cross is complex, and so, we must accept the power of the cross by faith, because we, as humans, can never fully grasp everything that happened on Calvary: a mystery whereby death is overcome, sins are forgiven, and eternal life becomes a reality. On the cross, God demonstrated this: that weakness defeats strength; wisdom is disguised as foolishness; and God's presence is camouflaged as absence. God had a plan for the cross – to identify with all the brokenness of this world, so people would know God is not against them, but rather God is with them. To deliver that message God chose the cross, the worst and most dreaded form of death, through which to work his power of love.

In the power of the cross, there is redemption and transformation, and there is also revelation. *'There is more of the true identity of God on the cross than any place else in the history of humankind.'* God on the cross is a paradox, a contradiction. Even Jesus himself cried out, *'My God, my God, why have you forsaken me?'* Yet, in time, we have come to believe that when God seemed to be most absent, he was actually the most present.

God on the cross proves God is present in the most God-forsaken places in the world; God is where you least expect God to be. The cross teaches us there is no place, no situation where God is not willing to meet us and bear with us. So the addict, the refugee, the criminal, the starving, the dying, and all of us ordinary people living ordinary lives will know that God feels our pain.

There is a story of a little boy by the name of Jake who got permission from his mom to go to the corner store. He didn't come back and didn't come back. His mom was getting both irritated and worried. Finally, when he arrived, his mother's tone of voice said it all: *'Where have you been?'* Jake explained, *'The boy down the block crashed his brand new bike, so I stopped to help him.'* His mother replied, *'How can you help? You are just a little boy; you don't know anything about fixing bikes.'* Jake replied, *'I sat on the curb and cried with him'.*

Our God is a God of empathy and compassion, but he does more than sit on the curb and cry with us. Ours is a God of transformation, who by the power of the cross can turns things around – war into peace, evil into good, hate into love, and death into life. Life and death collide on the cross. Death appears to win on that Friday afternoon, but we all know that death is not the end of the story. The resurrection of Jesus on Easter morning is evidence that God was more active at the cross than any place else in human history.

AMEN.

Scripture: John 19:1-30
Good Friday, April 18, 2014
Lake Preston/North Preston Lutheran Church, Lake Preston, S.D.

EASTER

RESURRECTION HOPE

There was a chill in the air that first Easter morning as a thin salmon-colored streak of light pierced the grey sky. In the distance, silhouetted through morning mist, stood three empty crosses. The damp chill in the air matched the dampened spirits of the women who went to the tomb. They had cried their eyes out and were exhausted with grief.

This was the third day after Jesus was crucified, and it was their duty to come to the tomb and to prepare Jesus' body for a proper burial. On Friday, after they took him down from the cross, they had brought his body to the tomb without preparation, because preparation for burial couldn't be done on the Sabbath, and the Sabbath was approaching. Now, the women came to wash the dried blood off Jesus' body, to comb his matted hair, and to cover him with spices before wrapping him in linen. They also came to spend some final time with him, saying their last good-byes.

On the way to the tomb, they were probably wondering how they would roll the stone away. But, when they arrived, the stone was gone. The entrance to the tomb was open, so they walked in, expecting to find Jesus' body. There was no body; it was gone! How could that be? A corpse doesn't just vanish into thin air; there had to be an explanation. Immediately, two men appeared in dazzling clothes, asking, *'Why do you look for the living among the dead?'* The women were terrified! Who wouldn't be terrified?

First, there was a missing body, and then two angels. Their response on that first Easter was not quite the same as our Easter greeting of '*Alleluia! Christ is risen!*' This was the first Easter: death to them was just that – death. Death was the end of the road, a blank wall, separation from God. The Jews had a vague idea about the resurrection, but that was for all people on Judgment Day at some distant time in the future. No one expected the resurrection, even though Jesus had mentioned to the disciples that he would be rising from the dead on the third day. They didn't 'get it,' because the resurrection was such a strange, new idea it simply didn't compute.

This is our Easter; do we 'get it'? Do we 'get' that the resurrection is a once in the history of humankind miracle from God that forever changes everything? Things will never be the same again because God has intervened in our lives in a startling new way. The world said 'no' to Jesus –'no' to his preaching, 'no' to his healing the sick, 'no' to his spending time with sinners, and punctuated that 'no' by hanging him on the cross. God's response was 'yes' to everything Jesus did. 'Yes' to Jesus fulfilling his mission, 'yes' to loving the least, 'yes' to feeding the hungry. God punctuated his 'yes' with the resurrection. When God raised Jesus of Nazareth from the dead, God declared him his anointed, the Christ, and put his stamp of approval on everything Jesus did.

The resurrection is the cornerstone belief of Christianity. Without the resurrection, we would have no savior and no church. That is why we make such a big deal out of Easter – with music, flowers, and greetings. When the women went to the tomb to prepare Jesus' body, they were focused on the past, Jesus' crucifixion, and the loss of their master. They went seeking a corpse, and found evidence of life. Because of the resurrection, we can focus on the future – and our own resurrection. Death becomes the gateway to eternal life – that is the resurrection hope we cling to at the time of death. But, resurrection is as much for the living as it is for the dead.

When Jesus rose from the dead, his Spirit, the Holy Spirit, was let loose in the world to continue the work he had begun. We will never follow Jesus down the dusty roads of Galilee or sit at his feet as he teaches, but by way of his Spirit, he is among us still. '*For the same Spirit that raised Jesus from the dead lives in us.'*[1] With his Spirit in us, life is full of possibilities, because we have a living Lord.

If Easter says anything, it says that Jesus will always be with us in Spirit. The pyramids of Egypt are famous because they contain the mummified bodies of ancient Egyptian kings. Westminster Abbey in London is renowned because in it rest the bodies of British nobles. Arlington National Cemetery is revered as the honored resting place of our brave American heroes. However, the Garden Tomb in Jerusalem is famous because it is empty. We don't celebrate the *memory* of a risen savior; we celebrate the *presence* of a risen savior.

Resurrection gives us hope, and limitless possibilities in our lives. The resurrection does not promise us smooth sailing, or life in a rose garden, or living happily ever after. It does promise us the presence of Jesus to help us keep our faith in fearful times, to give us peace when in pain, and to strengthen us for the struggles of life. Resurrection assures us that God has the final word and that gives us hope.

Little did the frightened women at the tomb realize they were witnesses to a history-changing, earth-shattering event. The resurrection of Jesus Christ set the world on a new path that showed us our God cannot be defeated by death, that showed us our God is the source of full, abundant life, beginning now and continuing into eternity. Thanks be to God for giving us resurrection hope. Alleluia! Alleluia!

AMEN.

Luke 24:1-12
Easter Sunday, March 27, 2016
Bethlehem Lutheran Church, Rockford, Ill.

PEACE – PERFECT PEACE

'We all dance on the wheel of time... where death & dying are as certain as birth & being.... Hellos & goodbyes are part of the fabric of life.'

Each of us has a personal style for saying 'goodbye.' Some people won't actually say 'goodbye;' they say something like 'so long' or 'talk to you later.' Some simply hug and use no words, while others want to say it all. Goodbyes are not easy.

For years I lived on the East Coast, and went home to see my mother in western Iowa. When it was time to leave, she would give me a long hug and say, *'Oh, I wish you didn't have to go, wish you didn't live so far away.'* Then, as I drove away, she would stand at the end of the sidewalk waving pensively. When she reached her late 80s, her goodbyes changed. She would hug me and say, *'You live in D.C. Anything can happen, and I'm getting old – we might not see each other again here on earth.'* As I drove away, there was no more pensive waving; she would turn toward the house and start tending her flowers.

Yes, goodbyes can be hard. Jesus did more than simply tell his disciples goodbye – he gave instructions, he made promises, and he gave them the priceless gift of peace. Jesus promised that although he would not be physically present as he had been in the past, his Spirit would come to continue the work he had begun. The Holy

Spirit would remind the disciples of everything Jesus had said to them while gently pulling them into the future.

We 21st century disciples live in the presence of the promised Holy Spirit. The Holy Spirit, Jesus' Spirit, is God in the present for us, here and now. When Scripture comes alive and past events engage us rather than remain passive – it is the work of the Holy Spirit. When we feel that gentle urge to pray, have an 'ah-ha!' moment, feel a twinge of conviction or feel our hearts soften – it is the Holy Spirit. When we are part of a coincidence or get an intuitive nudge – it is the Holy Spirit.

The Holy Spirit comes where invited, giving the final gift Jesus gave his disciples – the gift of peace. *'Peace I give to you – my peace I give to you. I do not give as the world gives. Do not let your hearts be troubled. And do not let them be afraid.'* That same peace is available to us now.

When we think of peace, we think of a world free of war and conflict. We all value this worldly peace. However, the peace of Christ is something entirely different. The peace of Christ is not just experienced when our lives are in a state of harmony, there is money in the bank, or the kids are doing well. The peace of Christ is possible when everything is going wrong, when things are upset and life seems to be going to hell in a handbag. The peace Christ gives is not as the world gives; it is a deep sustaining peace, anchored in God. Christ's peace doesn't say, 'Everything will be OK,' or 'Life will be like it was or the way we want it to be.' Christ's peace says things are in God's hands and God knows what is best for us. This enables us to trust God will work through all things for our benefit.

Nature gives us a good illustration. The surface of the sea is often agitated with fierce storms, pounding waves, and driving winds, but below the surface there is a part of the sea that never stirs; it is called the 'cushion of the sea.' Those who study the sea have found the remains of animals and vegetable life that have not been disturbed for hundreds and thousands of years. Treasure hunters are also amazed because the bounty from sunken ships from years ago lays quietly in this silent tomb, unbothered by the storms on the surface. The peace of God is that internal calm which, like the cushion of the sea, lies far too deep to be reached by any worldly trouble or disturbance. When we enter the peace of God and the peace of God enters us, we know God's eternal calm.

In my many years as a pastor, I have heard people say, '*I don't understand it. Things aren't going well, I have problem after problem, yet, I am at peace.*' That is precisely what Jesus is talking about, because with the gift of peace that passes all understanding, hearts are not troubled and we are not afraid. *Christ's peace is a peace that the world cannot give: a peace the world cannot take away.*

This perfect peace is ours for the asking. With hearts open, we invite the Spirit, '*Come, Holy Spirit Come – fill me with your peace.*' When this peace – the peace of Christ – comes, troubled hearts and fears disappear.

AMEN.

Scripture: John 14:23-29
May 1, 2016
Bethlehem Lutheran Church, Rockford, Ill.

PENTECOST

HEIRS BY ADOPTION

To whom are you in debt? Who do you owe? When you attend church in your Sunday finery, who holds the title to your car or the deed to your house? Debt is the American way of life; we may not like it, but it is the norm. In year 2000, the average American credit card debt was $8,000. Truth is, without debt and a credit rating, you might be at more of a disadvantage than with debt.

We must remember that there are debts other than financial ones. There are debts of gratitude to our forefathers and mothers who built this nation, to the parents who raised us, to the educational institutions which taught us, and to our home churches which nourished us in the faith. We don't mind these debts of gratitude; we count them as blessings. We respond joyfully to their demands, living our lives to bring honor to the family name or the institution from which we graduated or by being patriotic. We are fully aware we will never be able to pay some debts in full.

Paul, in Romans, Chapter 8, reminds us there is another debt we can never pay in full. That debt is to God, who has adopted us, named us as his children, given us a share of his spirit and the promise of salvation. We were 'up for adoption,' and God put his claim on us, through Jesus Christ, at our baptism when the sign of the cross was made on our foreheads, and we were called 'child of God'.

To be called a 'child of God' speaks to our true identity, not just to a label that we wear. There are many labels in our lives, such as age or profession or marital status, and they change according to our situation. Labels come and go, but 'child of God' is permanent, because it speaks to the relationship God has chosen to have with us. It is God's choice to love us and care for us, as a father would a child. So our identity as 'child of God' speaks to the source of being and salvation's destiny.

Adoption as 'children of God' means we are granted the full rights and privileges of belonging to a family with all the good and bad, joys and sorrows, that family life brings. Adoption gives us all the rights that come with belonging to a family to which one does not belong to naturally. We are not born Christians, but rather, by faith, we become Christians. Adoption gives us status as 'children of God' – heirs of God and joint heirs with Christ. What a gift! What grace!

One of the privileges of being in a family is intimacy – to simply be at home, where we can take off our shoes or raid the refrigerator without asking permission. Likewise, family communication is intimate; nicknames and inside jokes are shared with Mom and Dad or siblings. This is also true with our heavenly family; we can call God, 'Abba God' or 'Daddy God.' How wonderful to have a place so close to God! We are not stepchildren or distant cousins twice removed. No, we are part of the family of God. We are adopted, rooted in God's family tree through the very branch that bore the cross.

God has said, 'Yes' to us by claiming us as his own; now, we say 'Yes' in return. *'For all who are led by the Spirit of God are children of God'.* To be a child of God is to be shaped and molded by the Spirit, transformed to live in the Spirit. In his Letter to the Romans, Paul writes, *'You are in the Spirit since the Spirit of God dwells in you. ... If the Spirit of God who raised Jesus from the dead by the resurrection power dwells in you, then God who raised Christ from the dead will give life to our mortal bodies also through his Spirit that dwells in you.'* You have resurrection power in you, now – and you need it.

Paul says there is a war within us, between the flesh that kills through sin and the Spirit that gives us life with freedom and hope. Paul seems to suggest the choices between flesh and Spirit are clear. Truthfully, I find the majority of life choices more ambiguous. What does 'life in the Spirit' look like? Would you eat Bran Flakes instead of Cheerios? Would you take public transportation rather than drive? Does every life choice boil down to flesh or Spirit? After all, we spend the majority of our time doing the routine things – we eat, we sleep, we work, we play, we love. I believe the deciding factor is that choosing for the flesh increases the focus on 'me' - *my* self-worth, *my* self-satisfaction, and *my* self-centeredness. Choosing for the Spirit takes the focus off me and puts it on others to benefit them. So, no matter if you are feeding the baby in middle of the night, cleaning the house, chatting at a cocktail party or crossing the street it is the focus that matters – myself or others?

About now you are probably thinking that 'living in the Spirit' must be exhausting because we have to think of it all the time. Not so, to be shaped and molded by the Spirit means our attitude is transformed, and it becomes for us a new way of life. I am convinced that there is a vast store house of Spirit we never tap into. In many ways, we try hard at being Christian, and doing the right thing. Yet, we often fail. Instead we need to allow ourselves to be empowered by the Spirit. It is only through the power of the Spirit that we can forgive or love our enemies or bless those who curse us. We cannot do that on our own.

Think of it this way: You win the lottery of $1,000,000. They deliver it to you and you say, 'I don't need that much; $50 will do just fine, so you can take the rest back'. Can you imagine that? Well, that is what we do daily when we settle for spiritual crumbs, and continue to live in the flesh by hating or whining or worrying rather than enjoying the Spiritual banquet that makes life full and abundant.

In our baptism, God has claimed us as children of God and bound us to our Lord Jesus Christ. When we claim the full inheritance that God has in store for us, then the Spirit of Jesus comes into our lives to help us live beyond our human limitations. Believing this should make us cry out, 'Come Holy Spirit, come! Fill us with resurrection power so that we can be all God created us to be.'

Come Holy Spirit, Come.

Amen.

Scripture: Romans 8: (9-13), 14-17.
Pentecost Sunday, May 19, 2002,
Lutheran Church of the Reformation, Washington, D.C.

TIME AFTER PENTECOST

TRUST AND OBEY

There is a legend about Jesus from those quiet years of his life, before he started his public ministry. The legend claims that Jesus, the carpenter, was a master yoke-maker in Nazareth. People came from miles around for Jesus, son of Joseph, to craft a hand-carved yoke for their oxen. Customers would arrive with their teams of oxen, and Jesus would spend considerable time with them, measuring the team for height and width, measuring the space between the animals, and the size of their shoulders. Within a week, the team would be brought back, and the newly-crafted yoke would be slipped over the oxen's shoulders. Then, any needed adjustments would be made.

In Matthew's Gospel, Jesus speaks of yokes; he urges us, *'take my yoke upon you – for my yoke is easy and my burden light.'* We must not be misled by the word 'easy.' In Greek, the root word for 'easy' is interpreted as 'well-fitting.' The yoke Jesus invites us to take is one that is specifically fitted to us, making the burden light. The yoke does not rub or cause us to develop sore spirits, because it is a yoke shared with an empowering Christ.

I imagine Abraham could tell us a thing or two about being yoked with God. God had Abraham's number when he called upon him to leave Ur, and father a new nation with descendants as plentiful as grains of sand on the seashore. Years rolled by; still, there was no son for Abraham and Sarah, and doubts arose. Abraham, who was

HEART TO HEART

not especially patient, twice passed Sarah off as his sister when famine forced them to travel in foreign lands. But, God saved them despite their foolishness. Then, they tried to offer substitutes for a son of their own who could be an heir to Abraham: his servant, Eliezer, and the offspring of Sarah's handmaiden, Hagar. God refused their substitutes. Abraham and Sarah laughed as they waited, but when the geriatric couple was 100- and 90-years-old respectively, Isaac was born! What joy! The wait had been long and the wait had been hard, but the wait was worth it, because God did what God said. God had proven to be trustworthy.

Isaac grew, as little boys do, and then God made a demanding request of Abraham. *'Take your son, your only son Isaac, whom you love, and offer him as a burnt offering on a mountain that I shall show you.'* This is an incredibly troubling story unless we look at it in the context of Abraham's day and not ours. It is also an incredibly beneficial story, because we can learn from Abraham what it means to be yoked in trust with God. This story, for all its intensity, gives only a few facts; it reveals none of Abraham's feelings or thoughts; it provides no evidence of Sarah's involvement. Did she know that her son was a potential sacrifice? Human sacrifice was not an uncommon custom in some Canaanite tribes, but the religion of the patriarchs was radically different from surrounding cultures. The God of Abraham was a God of compassion and caring. God showed that caring when he spoke to Abraham, *'take your son, your only son Isaac whom you love.'* With those words, you can hear how God felt about both Abraham and Isaac. The God of Abraham was a radically different god than the cruel, capricious god of the Canaanites.

But, sometimes God does come across as unreasonable and demanding. An unreasonable God might ask a young woman to deliver her firstborn in a cowshed. A demanding God might ask Noah to quit planting crops to build an ark, and then collect two of every species from spiders to sparrows to put in that ark. Trusting a demanding God can be a challenge. Unreasonable, yes, God can be that. But unreasonable according to whom? What may seem unreasonable to us with our myopic vision may not be unreasonable to our God who has cosmic vision.

Abraham must have had an incredible relationship with God. God spoke. Abraham obeyed. By then, God had proven himself trustworthy, so although what God asked of Abraham didn't make sense, Abraham knew God could be trusted.

When I read about God calling Abraham, I find myself reflecting on my own call to go to seminary. When God speaks to me – yes, God does speak to me – the message comes with incredible clarity of thought, accompanied by a feeling of urgency to do what I have been instructed. So, when I got the call to go to seminary, it made no difference that my husband and I had a home full of foster kids, that we were building a house, that I had a really good nursing job, but not the college degree necessary for admission to seminary. By the time I left for seminary two years later, all the obstacles had been worked out. I trusted this God-given message of the call because other messages like it had proven trustworthy in the past. Trust is built on trustworthy experiences.

The issue here is that when Abraham heard from God, he was willing to obey – maybe not a 'rah, rah!' willingness, but still willing. My mental picture of Abraham, as he prepared for the trip to the mountain, is of him dragging his feet, walking slowly, as though the weight of the world was on his shoulders. By moving slowly, he knew he could hear if God called again. He was willing to go and do when he didn't have a clue about the outcome. Abraham was willing to say, 'here I am,' rather than hide under a rock. Abraham might not have understood what God commanded him to do, but being a man of faith, he was prepared to do whatever God commanded. His response was simply to trust and obey.

There is another clue to Abraham's faith. On the third day, when he saw the mountain in the distance, he said to his servant, *'Stay here with the donkey; the boy and I will go over there. We will worship, and then we will come back to you.'* We will come back to you. To me that says Abraham did not know the way out, but he believed that if he were obedient, God would provide a way out as part of a bigger plan. God did not let Abraham down.

This lesson started with God testing Abraham. I think we could say that Abraham passed the test. I dare say a different Abraham went up the mountain than came down from the mountain. It has been said Satan tempts us to bring out the worst in us; God tests us to bring out the best in us. Maybe you are thinking you are sure glad God doesn't test you like he tested Abraham. In truth, every day we are tested in multiple small ways, which prepare us for the moment in our lives when we will make our personal trek up Moriah's mountain to see if we will pay the ultimate price for what conscience compels us to do.

How much do you trust God? Do you trust God enough to admit there are some things you need to sacrifice on the altar for sake of your relationship with God? Do you trust God enough to feel confident that God can provide a better solution to your problem, whatever it is, than you have in mind? Our God is trustworthy! On the mountain when Abraham had the knife raised over Isaac, God called to Abraham from heaven, *'Abraham, Abraham. Do not lay your hand on the boy – for now, I know that you fear God.'* God provided a ram in the thicket.

God's trustworthiness continues through the centuries. For God did what he stopped Abraham from doing – he sacrificed his son. Jesus became for us the lamb in the thicket, who forgives our sins and is our salvation. Abraham was asked to pay a great price, to sacrifice his son to ensure the covenant God made with him, but God provided a way out. Then, God paid the great price for us by sacrificing his son. It is through Jesus' life, death, and resurrection God that provides for us fullness of life on earth and an eternal home in heaven. Doesn't this prove that he is trustworthy of our obedience?

Scripture: Genesis 22: 1-14; Matthew 11:28-30
(Date Unknown)
Lutheran Church of the Reformation, Washington, D.C.

POLITICS OF COMPASSION

Around Memorial Day, there are a lot of war stories in the news. One from the Vietnam era stuck with me. That would have been the late 1960s, and battlefield trauma medicine was at a far different stage than it is now. When casualties were brought in from the battlefield – and there were so many of them – they were put in body bags, and went directly to the make-shift morgue. At one, a private, who worked in the morgue, had a fear: *What if a soldier in one of those bags wasn't really dead*? After all, he had gone directly from the battlefield to the morgue. So, every time a body arrived in the morgue, he unzipped the bag, took a blunt instrument and thrust it along the bottom of the soldier's foot to see if it triggered the plantar reflex, an indication that life remained. He did that on one seemingly-dead soldier, and got a response. He tried the sole of the other foot and got a response. He yelled for the doctor, 'We *have a live one here!'* Alive that soldier was and remained; he was interviewed by a TV reporter for the story I saw. The soldier lived because of a private who worried, *'What if the dead weren't really dead?'*

When Jesus saw the dead young man and his mother approach, surrounded by a crowd of weeping and wailing mourners, on their way to the cemetery, he might have thought, *'What if he dies; she too will die far too soon.'* Jesus didn't see just one death; he saw two. Scripture reads, *'he was his mother's only son, and she was a widow.'* His death meant she was doomed to an early death, too, because women had to rely on their husbands and sons for identity and security. Without a male to rely on, she was at the mercy of the community, and that usually meant an early death. Jesus knew all of this, and had compassion on her. What a beautiful statement that is: *'He had compassion on her.'*

Compassion is a feeling that is extremely visceral, originating in the gut or womb. The head intellectualizes, and the heart feels empathy or pity. Compassion is 'I feel for you' or 'I feel your pain.' We might feel compassion for those we love, but Jesus felt it for strangers. Jesus was demonstrating for us a down-to-earth God as he acted with compassion, and reflected a God who feels for us. The Jewish religious system was based on the politics of purity where everything was clean or unclean, 'Be *holy as God is holy.'*[1] Into this religious culture, Jesus introduced the politics of compassion – 'be compassionate as God is compassionate.' To God, compassion is more important than holiness. In this story, Jesus crosses the boundaries of clean and unclean, life and death, women and men, to offer compassion.

When Jesus raised the young man from the dead, *"fear seized them all,'* and the crowd glorified God. They saw a new day dawning. The crowd following Jesus probably remembered Elijah, who raised a widow's son to authenticate his role as prophet, and prayed down God's power to do it.[2] Jesus, as prophet, did more; his motivation was compassion and his Word was all the power he needed. Elijah provided the backstory that allowed Jesus to be identified with God, and to be seen as the One through whom God would look favorably on all his people.

What a wonderful miracle this was! In reviving the young man and returning him to his mother, Jesus restored two lives, not just one. However, this story, as wonderful as it is, might touch a raw spot in our souls. The Bible is full of miracles; however, we would like to see more miracles in the lives of the people for whom we pray. Sure, we hear of the occasional tumor that disappears, or the heart that heals on its own, but we would like to see more. Perhaps, this sounds unappreciative – wanting more miracles when we already live in the age of Modern Medicine where God works through science, technology, doctors and nurses. We are so surrounded by mundane miracles that we accept them as normal. There is a reason life expectancy in the United States is 74 years. There is a reason seniors are the fastest growing segment of our population. We are all the recipients of the miracles of Modern Medicine.

Still, we are left with the haunting questions about unanswered prayer. When we ask God for healing, perhaps God's focus is much broader than ours. God sees us in a holistic way, and perhaps the condition of our soul is of more concern to God than our cancer or arthritis. Perhaps, the prayer we thought was unanswered, was answered, but beyond our physical sight.

I will never forget the phone call; the voice on the other end said, *'Pray for me – they found brain cancer.'* I knew John was having bad headaches and had gone to the doctor; the doctors quickly discovered a brain tumor. John's family had a strong history of cancer. John was 39, the father of a preschool daughter and two elementary-aged sons. Doctors tried every conceivable treatment, and repeated surgeries, but nothing stopped the very aggressive cancer. So, John willingly agreed to new experimental medications and treatments at the National Institute of Health, fully aware they wouldn't help him, but might help someone else in the future. John came to church and gave his testimonial. Eloquently, he thanked – yes, thanked – God for what the rest of us saw as a painful ordeal. He was thankful, because his pending death had elevated his faith and awakened him to a new level of spiritual life. John was no stranger to church: a preacher's kid (PK), a Sunday School teacher, an active member. Fortified by his faith, he counted himself blessed, even as he left behind a grieving family and community. Our prayers for John's return to health weren't answered, but John admittedly received far more than he could have ever asked or imagined.

There are so many things about the providence of God we will never understand. But, by faith, we do know the most important things. Ours is a God of compassion who suffers with us and beside us. The cross of Jesus is evidence that God feels our pain. Our God can work through all things, both known or unknown, through laws of nature and human choice, to achieve his purpose and our benefit.

We must remember: Our God has provided the ultimate miracle for each of us. The only miracle that really matters is the Resurrection. We, like the young man, are as good as dead in trespasses and sin, but the compassion of God, shown in the power of Jesus, promises all of us new life in the Resurrection.

AMEN.

Scripture: Luke 7:11-17
June 5, 2016
Bethlehem Lutheran Church, Rockford, Ill.

FINDING OURSELVES IN THE DITCH

With this reflection, we consider the universally-loved Gospel story of the Good Samaritan. You have probably heard this story so often your ears go on auto pilot when it is read. Time has tamed the impact of it, and repetition has domesticated it. When it was first heard, the story of the Good Samaritan was subversive and outrageous. So, shake off the old ideas you have about the Good Samaritan, and consider it as if for the first time.

The story starts with a young lawyer testing Jesus: *'What must I do to inherit eternal life?'* Jesus returns the test: *'What is written in the law?'* The young lawyer knows the answer: *'Love the Lord your God with all your heart, your mind, and your soul, and your neighbor as yourself.'* The lawyer passed the test. Jesus responds: *'Do this and you will live.'* You sense the exchange is almost over, and the lawyer is walking away. Then he has an after-thought and returns for clarification: 'Who is my neighbor?'

This is not a new question; in fact, it was a hot topic, widely discussed by rabbis. *'Love of neighbor as self'* is quoted all the way back to Leviticus 19:18. Neighbors were primarily seen as citizens of Israel like themselves. However, Leviticus 19:34 adds a new twist to this understanding when it says, *'you shall love the alien as yourself.'* So, the question of 'who is your neighbor?' was very much alive.

Some drew the circle that contained neighbors very tightly – to exclude others; some drew the circle very loosely – to include others. However, everyone agreed the circle never included one group – the Samaritans. So, Jesus addresses the neighbor question with a parable.

A 'certain man' was going from Jerusalem to Jericho. That was a sixteen-mile trip, with a drop in elevation of 3600 feet. The road was a dark, twisting and treacherous path, lined with caves where robbers lived. A certain man fell into the hands of thieves; he was beaten, stripped, and left half dead. We don't know if the 'certain man' was Jew or Gentile, rich or poor, young or old. We only know he was stripped and left naked, nearly dead, and not able to speak. Passersby would have had no clue as to his nationality.

Imagine that you were that 'certain man' who had been in Jerusalem on business, and you wanted to get home to your wife and kids. You know better than to travel that road alone – it wasn't called the Bloody Way for nothing – but you decided to take your chances rather than spend another night in Jerusalem. As you hurried along the road, you looked nervously left and right; you listened for strange sounds, and then it happened. The robbers jumped you, beat you nearly to death, tore off your clothes, took anything of value you carried, and left you to die on the side of road. Imagine: you are lying there; it is now nearly dark, and the evening chill is in the air. One of your eyes is swollen shut; there is a metallic taste of blood in your mouth; you can feel some broken teeth, broken like your ribs that are causing you great pain as breathing is getting more difficult. You feel death is near.

Then, you hear footsteps. Through your good eye, you see the robe and insignia of a temple priest. You think, 'help has arrived!' Priests know they are to help people in need. Little did you know that your need was not the issue; the issue for the priest was touching you, which would make him unclean. To your dismay, you hear the footsteps leave. Later, who knows how much later, because you slip in and out of consciousness, you hear more footsteps. Hope springs again. You see the robe and staff of a Levite; he is unsure if you are dead or alive, so he also takes a pass on helping you. To touch you would mean he would lose a week's work; besides, he doesn't have time to be concerned with you. The Levite and priest were both righteous and religious men, God's servants. If they won't help, who will? Death is inevitable.

You know you are dying; then, you hear footsteps again. You see the man is wearing the clothes of a Samaritan. You think he will probably finish you off just for the fun of it, so you prepare for the worst. Then, you hear the creak of the leather water skin being opened, and you feel the cool water as it is being poured through your broken and bleeding lips, and splashed gently on your face. Then, the man tears off a piece of his own garment to bind up your wounds after cleaning them with oil and wine. Then, painstakingly, he lifts you to the back of his donkey to take you to a safe place.

When Jesus finished the story, I imagine the original crowd was aghast – a Samaritan was the hero? That couldn't be! Samaritans were always the bad guys; in fact, the robbers were probably Samaritans. Jesus' question summed it up, *'Which of these three was a neighbor to the man who fell into the hands of robbers?'* The lawyer replied, *'The one who showed mercy.'* No one could argue – the Samaritan was the hero. Then, Jesus gives us one of the most difficult assignments ever, 'Go and do likewise.'

Through telling this parable, Jesus very skillfully shifted the focus of the debate from defining who our neighbors are – what they look like, or where they are from – to us and how we relate to people. Do we show mercy? In life, we can't choose our family, but we do choose our friends, and most of us would like to choose the neighbors we live near and our co-workers, but generally that is not our choice. The only choice we get is how we will react to our neighbors, to the people who cross our path or lie in the ditch next to the road.

I spent years teaching health classes in a job-readiness program in the inner city of Washington, DC. Each class had from fifteen to twenty African American men who were tough, streetwise ex-offenders, trying to get their lives back on track. One topic I taught was racial stress; we had lively discussions because I was a safe person to question. I fielded questions such as 'how do white people think?' One day a student politely, but bluntly, asked *'Are you a racist?'* Am I a racist? There was no way I could soft-pedal or take a pass on that question. Everyone was waiting for my response; all eyes in the room were focused on me. My mind was racing as I took a deep breath.

'Yes, I think I am a racist. I don't want to be a racist, but I think I am one. I think racism is part of the tribal-tendency of original sin where we prefer our own kind and feel safer with others like us. I am constantly aware of my own racism, so I have to be on guard with how I respond. An incident led me to this conclusion: one day I was carrying a purse over my shoulder and met an African American man I didn't know on the street. Instinctively, without thinking, I automatically clutched my purse tighter. I didn't want to respond that way, but it was instinctive. That alarmed me, and made me think that deep down there is some racism in me – even if I don't want it to be there, it is there.'

The room was dead quiet. I realized that what I said sounded like confession. From the back of the room came a word of absolution spoken by a most unlikely person. It came from Alfonzo, an ex-offender body builder, whose oiled muscles rippled under his tank top. He stood up and said, *'That's OK pastor, I understand. We are all human. Don't be so hard on yourself. Sometimes even us Black guys are afraid when we see others we don't know.'* That was a Good Samaritan moment for me: I, the white clergy woman who absolves sin, was in the ditch. But Alfonzo, a Black man on the bottom of the social ladder, offered me absolution and understanding. He was the Good Samaritan.

We can't understand this story until we see ourselves in the ditch – not as the one saving someone else, but as the one needing to be saved. God rescued us through the saving grace of Jesus Christ when we were covered with our sin and mortality. Our wounds have been cleansed with forgiveness; we have been splashed with baptismal waters, fed with bread and wine, and taken to a safe and caring place in the heart of God. God did not pass us by. Now, out of our love for God, we are called to do likewise.

Go and do as God has done for you. Do not pass others by.

AMEN.

Scripture: Luke 10:25-37
July 10, 2016
Bethlehem Lutheran Church, Rockford, Ill.

PRAYER BEYOND ALL PRAYERS

Life is filled with teachable moments – those opportune times that arise when a learner, either child or adult, wants to know more and connect it with whatever else they already know. Teachable moments aren't predictable; they are a spontaneous occurrence, so the teacher or parent must be ready to respond.

Luke's Gospel provides a good example of a teachable moment with the disciples. They sensed there was more they needed to know about prayer, since Jesus' style of praying was different from others. Jewish prayers in the first century were ritualistic prayers of the hours. They prayed specific words at specific times. When Jesus prayed, he would withdraw to a mountain or the lakeshore, and return refreshed and energized. The disciples also knew Jesus was harsh on the scribes and Pharisees who prayed exhibition-style prayers on street corners, using a lot of fluff and flowery words.

What the disciples received in response to their request, *'Lord teach us to pray,'* was the Lord's Prayer, a prayer that is incredibly brief and specific. The Lord's Prayer takes us as close to Jesus' spiritual life, and his message of the Kingdom, as we can get. Jesus teaches the disciples by expanding their concept of prayer from prayers of repetition and ritual to prayers of relationship. He makes that transition with the simple words, *'Our Father.'* Those words introduce an attitude of intimacy and trust: we are children and God is our father. The phrase, 'our Father,' – not 'my Father' – sets the stage for the family of God, living in community.

Jesus follows this opening with two petitions that give God priority:

- *Hallowed be thy name* – acknowledging God's honor and glory.
- *Your Kingdom come* – inviting into our lives God's hope to renew the whole world, and to bring it back into its original state.

After addressing the importance of God, the prayer moves on to address our human need for daily bread, for forgiveness of our sins, and for help to overcome temptation. We need to be aware that in the Lord's Prayer we are submitting ourselves to the Kingdom of God, which is God's design for the world, God's will for the world. We are agreeing to a shift our priorities; we are no longer the center of the universe. God is first, others are next, we are last.

I love the Lord's Prayer, as I am sure many of you do to, but sometimes I am concerned we know it so well we pray it on autopilot; the words fly out of our mouths, but are not connected with our hearts. Our minds are thinking about lunch or the weather while we spew the words that Jesus gave us. But on the other hand, its familiarity is also a blessing; it is a prayer of solidarity for Christians, even as it is the outline for Christian living.

When my son, Chris, came to us as a six-year-old foster child, we always said grace before meals and we took turns. One night it was Chris' turn. With eyes pinched shut, hands tightly grasped, he prayed, *'Dear God,* (long, long pause*) Help, help, help. Amen.'* It was the most fervent prayer I have ever heard, but I still do not know why Chris needed help. However, he demonstrated the essentials for prayer: brief and basic.

Prayer, as Jesus taught it, focuses on relationship, not results. That calls for an adjustment in our thinking, because we want answers to our prayers. Why pray if we don't get answers? Be clear, God always answers our prayers. Answers sometimes come as 'yes.' Sometimes they come as 'no' – even Paul and Jesus got 'no-es.' Sometimes the answer is 'wait' or 'you have got to be kidding me.'

(Haven't we all prayed foolish prayers that we were glad weren't answered?)

The time between asking and receiving is important. That is the relationship time when the Holy Spirit molds and shapes us. Prayer changes things – no question – it might be the situation or it might be me. Too often, we go to God acting as his advisor, telling God what to do rather than asking God to do what is best in this situation. When someone says to me, 'I don't know what to pray for,' I know that is good, because then – as we lift the person or situation to God – we let God be God. Prayer changes things; prayer changes us. Let me offer you a Serenity Prayer rewrite: "*God grant me the serenity to accept the people I cannot change, the courage to change the only one I can, and the wisdom to know that person is me.'[1]*

Jesus then illustrates the point of relationship with a parable. A man goes to a friend's house at midnight and asks for bread to feed a traveling friend who just arrived. The friend, his family and animals were bedded down for the night, with the doors locked. However, because of the man's persistence and friendship, he is given the bread that he needs. With the parable, Jesus teaches us that if a friend will do that much, God our Father will do much more for those who ask for the Holy Spirit.

Then Jesus continues teaching about prayer with this: '*Ask, it will be given you; search, and you will find; knock, and the door will be opened to you.'* This sounds like an absolute guarantee, doesn't it? No, this is not an open-ended offer which will ensure we will receive our most delicious dreams and desires. Jesus' point is this: in relationship, we can ask with boldness – as long as it is part of God's will and the Kingdom. God, who takes delight in our prayers and desires our company, will gladly give us more than we either desire or deserve. We need only call on the promise in Luke 11:13: '*The heavenly Father will give the Holy Spirit to those who ask him'* – the Holy Spirit.

A little girl was kneeling beside her bed, reverently and prayerfully reciting the alphabet, '*A-B-C-D-E-F-G.'* Her grandfather overhead and interrupted. '*What are you doing?'* he asked. She replied, '*I'm saying my prayers, but I can't think of the exact words tonight, so I'm saying all the letters. God will put them in the right order for me, 'cause God knows what I'm thinking.'* She got the idea of being in relationship with God right.

When our sighs and groans are too deep for words, or when we are not sure how to pray,[2] God, who knows us intimately, will read our hearts. In the meantime, we can rely on the prayer above all prayers, the prayer that Jesus taught us – the Lord's Prayer.

AMEN.

Scripture: Luke 11:1-13
July 24, 2016
Bethlehem Lutheran Church, Rockford, Ill.

SEDUCTIVE WEALTH

Do you remember the children's story about Goldilocks and the Three Bears? Goldilocks was tripping through the forest, and tripped into the bears' cottage. The bears weren't home, but the table was set and the porridge poured. Goldilocks tasted the porridge – one bowl was too hot, another too cold, and the other, 'just right.' She sat in the bears' chairs – one was too small, another was too big, and the other was 'just right.' She slept in their beds – one was too soft, one was too hard, and the other one was 'just right.'

This children's story comes to mind as we ponder texts on wealth and possessions. If we possess too little, we are in poverty, and that can kill body and soul. If we possess too much, and are rich, that can be equally detrimental to our soul. However, we need to find a balance that is 'just right' – enough to meet our needs, yet not so much that our possessions control us.

Jesus was teaching the crowds when he was interrupted by a request: *'Teacher, tell my brother to divide the family inheritance with me.'* The backstory to his request was probably this: the oldest brother was entitled to two-thirds of the inheritance, primarily for the care of their parents in their old age. The younger brother was to get one-third, and the other siblings would have to fend for themselves. So, there was plenty of opportunity for dispute. It was common to ask a rabbi to settle disputes, so it would not have been unusual for the man to ask Jesus this question. But Jesus wanted no part of it. His response: '*Who set me to be a judge over you?*'

Instead of settling the dispute, Jesus went to the core cause of the dispute – greed. Greed is wanting more than we need. Greed can be a very slippery topic, and is easier to see in others than to recognize in ourselves. When think of greed, we think of those on Wall Street. When we think greed, we think of company CEOs who make thousands of times more than the average person on the plant's production line. Do you need more examples of greed? Watch the TV show, "American Greed." We don't have to look very far for examples of greed, because we live in a culture where the economy is fed by the desire for more. People are measured by how much they have. Our culture equates material wealth with the good life, money with personal worth, and consumption with satisfaction. That is why we are bombarded with advertisements trying to convince us to buy the latest technology, the newest car, or the most effective medicines.

Our culture also equates possessions with happiness. Yet, the United States – the richest nation in the world – ranks in the bottom ten percent (10%) of all nations for national happiness. The countries of Denmark, Norway, and Finland rank highest. Our culture promotes greed so subtly that we don't realize we are being taken in, until enough is never enough and we want more and more. There is a Roman proverb: *Money (and possessions) are like sea water, the more you drink, the more you want.*

Jesus brings this close to home with the parable of the farmer. The farmer had worked long and hard to get a great crop, a bumper crop; his barns could not contain the abundance of his crop. His solution was to tear down his barns and build bigger barns. That made sense, but the farmer's mistake was feeling safe and secure because of his prosperity. He said, '*I will say to my soul, "Soul you have ample goods laid up for many years; relax, eat, drink, be merry."*' He doesn't have a care in the world; his retirement plan was producing, his health benefits were good, and his investments were sound. But, God said to him, '*You fool! This very night your life is being demanded of you. And things you have prepared, whose will they* be? So it is with those who store treasures for themselves, but are not rich toward God.' The foolish farmer was rich in things, and poor of soul. The foolish farmer thought he had it made and he did by world standards. But, the farmer failed to realize that 'one's life does not consist in the abundance of possessions.' The poor foolish farmer thought he was in control of his own life, but he wasn't. God's visit made that perfectly clear.

This parable is a warning about wealth. Jesus is not against wealth. Remember, wealth is called a blessing in the Old Testament and still is a blessing. Jesus is warning us that wealth and possessions, 'things we store up as treasures for ourselves,' can create the illusion that our future is secure. That is not so. Our lives are on loan from God. We neither ask to be born nor know the number of our days. It does not matter if you are a bum or billionaire, royalty or a refugee – we all arrive in this world slippery, screaming, and red, and we leave this world cold, still, and dead.

To be rich in God is to trust God with our future security. Our future is secure because God, through Jesus Christ, transferred the riches of God to us on the cross, and with the resurrection, God made us heirs to eternal life and gave us salvation. How do we become rich in God? Richness in God is found in relationships, not in objects. It comes with acknowledging our natural inclination toward greed, acknowledging we are seduced by wealth. Richness in God comes from sharing what we have accumulated. Enjoy it now, and when your earthly life is over, share it with your family, but also share some with the family of God, especially those special to Jesus – the hungry, the naked, and the poor.

I once knew a woman who was so rich in God she didn't realize she was as poor as a church mouse; Alice was her name. Alice had been a dietary assistant for many years, and in her advanced years, she lived on a very small retirement and her Social Security. Whenever she went to a garage sale, she would stock up on small gift items so she was ready for any occasion that arose. I once took her with me to a Christmas party at the home of another church member, Fred, who had a lovely home in the country. Alice bought a $2.50 tie from a street vendor for Fred's hostess gift. Fred normally wore expensive ties that cost $75 or $100, but Alice's tie quickly became his favorite because of the love that came with it. Once, when I had a terrible head cold, Alice bought me a bag full of expensive over-the-counter drugs. Alice wished me well, and said she hoped my good health would soon return, and then she asked me to return to her the unused portion of the medications so she could use them on her next cold. The medicine was good, but my heart is warmed every time I think of her generosity – she was truly rich in God.

To be rich in God is to trust our future to God, and to use what we have been given on earth unselfishly for others. It is a blessing to be rich with things of the world, but that does not compare to being rich in God.

AMEN.

Scripture: Luke 12: 13-21
July 31, 2016
Bethlehem Lutheran Church, Rockford, Ill.

FEAR NOT LITTLE FLOCK

Have you had any telemarketer calls lately? Any promises of a vacation or cruise or the lowest credit card rates ever? These calls, recorded or real, are always made by enthusiastic callers who are far more impressed with your good fortune than you are. While they are giving you the pitch about your good luck, you are thinking, *'What is the catch?'* Then it is revealed – bring a paying passenger with you, tour the latest in time-shares, or transfer all your credit card debt. *'Momma didn't raise any dummies'* – if it sounds too good to be true, it probably is.

So, when we read in Luke's Gospel, *'Do not be afraid, little flock, for it is your Father's good pleasure to give you the Kingdom,'* you might have a tendency to hesitate and ask, *'What's the catch?'* Love is the catch, because it gives the Father good pleasure to give us – his beloved – the Kingdom. We give God pleasure – each one of us is one of God treasures; he takes delight in us, and wants what is best for us. That is why, for love's sake, God wants to give us the Kingdom.

God sent Jesus Christ into this world to become for us the key to the kingdom. As Jesus walked among us, sat at the table and ate with us, showed concern for the shunned or ugly, he became a walking, talking example of the Kingdom as peace, kindness, and compassion flowed from his very being. With his presence, the Kingdom of God was unfolding. It is a natural inclination for us to fill our hearts with the treasures of the world that can be held, things that are pretty and give pleasure, things that will eventually rust or decay or be broken. God sent Jesus to unlock our earthly hearts and make room for the lasting things that are eternal, instead of a stockpile of earthly things than are transient.

Jesus Christ exemplified how giving our God is. We are on the receiving end of a giving God. God gives – we receive. For us to receive what God has in store for us, we have to be ready. Jesus gives us advice on how to get ready. *"Sell all your belongings and give the money to the poor. Provide for yourself purses that won't wear out because they contain the riches of heaven."* This sounds like sheer madness when not seen through the eyes of faith. These blunt words are meant to attract our attention, and give us a wake-up call.

Jesus calls on us to detach from the treasures we hold in our hearts – to let go of them so with open hands and open hearts we can receive the Kingdom. Have you ever known someone who was terminally ill and started giving away their most prized possessions? The one who is dying tells friends they are welcome to choose from his or her possessions. At that point in their lives, they seem to know they don't need all the stuff they own, all the stuff that gave them pleasure. There is something more important as they prepare for the eternal.

This Gospel was very important in Jesus' day. There was a feeling of urgency, a belief that the world would soon end. Jesus was teaching his followers how to be prepared and ready in those uncertain times. He gives an example with servants who are dressed and ready, so when the master comes home and knocks on the door, they are prepared to open the it for him. But this tale of preparation has a twist to it: *'The master will fasten his belt and have them sit down to eat, and he will come and serve them.'* The message is this: *'You must be ready for the Son of Man is coming at an unexpected time.'* But, the Son of Man is no ordinary master, because he served us in his living and he served us in his dying.

The hour of our death or the end of the world – both are unknowns. Both cause us tremendous anxiety because the fear of death is the ultimate fear. Hear again the Good News: *'Have no fear, little flock, as the Kingdom of God liberates us from fear.'* Fear is re-placed by faith when we experience the Kingdom. The Kingdom offers peace, God's presence, assurance of eternal life and strength to meet any circumstance. Fear, anxiety and worry have always been the trademarks of humanity. And now, since we live in a world with a 24-hour news cycle, we have free-floating anxiety about things we didn't even know existed 10 years ago – things like Zika or ISIS. What will be next?

During the building of the Golden Gate Bridge, over the San Francisco Bay in 1936, construction fell badly behind schedule. Several workers had accidentally fallen from the scaffolding to their deaths. Engineers and administrators could find no solution to the costly delays, because the fearful laborers worked much slower, causing delays. Finally, someone suggested a gigantic net be hung under the bridge to catch anyone who fell. Despite the enormous cost, they invested in the net. After it was installed, progress proceeded smoothly – a worker or two fell, but they were saved by the net. Ultimately, all the time lost to fear was regained by replacing fear of falling with faith in the net.

Faith can overcome our fear; the Kingdom of God can liberate us from our fear. We have the choice. We can live in the grip of earthly fears and anxiety, or we can receive all that the Kingdom has to offer, including freedom from fear. The choice is ours – which will it be?

God's choice is clear – God wants to give us the Kingdom!

AMEN.

Scripture: Luke 12:32-40
August 7, 2016
Bethlehem Lutheran Church, Rockford, Ill.

THE GOOD NEWS OF TOUGH LOVE

When I preached my last sermon, I had hoped I could preach a feel-good sermon, one that was warm and fuzzy, with lots of talk of God's unconditional love. However, it was not to be so. That Sunday's Gospel was a hard gospel. Being true to the text, it was necessary to preach an edgy sermon about a stressed-out Jesus on tough love. I hope this hard gospel is as uncomfortable for you as it is for me.

This gospel makes us uncomfortable because we see Jesus in a different light. In this gospel, he confronts instead of comforts. We have seen an angry Jesus overturning tables in temple, and the snarly side of Jesus, making cutting comments to scribes and Pharisees. Our preferred Jesus is probably the loving, gentle Jesus, holding the children in his arms. In this gospel, we get a very human in-your-face kind of Jesus, one who rants about division instead of peace.

Don't we all know what it is to be stressed out? To feel torn and pulled by responsibilities and pressures beyond what we feel we can handle? Stress is one of the watchwords of our age, but stress has been around for a long time. Just like us, Jesus got stressed out, too: *'What stress I am under until this mission is complete.'* What is stressing Jesus? Jesus probably looked around and saw disciples who were dumb-founded and perplexed; they were not sure what was happening. There was also the crowd of curious and undecided folks, and probably some hangers-on, hoping to see another miracle. It is easy to understand how Jesus felt. After three years of hard work – preaching, teaching, and healing – he looked at those following him, shook his head, and realized he didn't have many followers to show for all his effort.

Jesus felt the urgency of not having much time left. He had come to bring the fire of judgment to the earth. Confronted by Jesus, people would either decide for him, and the Kingdom of God, or against him. The world's judgment against him would be his own baptismal fire of the crucifixion and his death. With that before him, and not many followers beside him, it is understandable why he felt stressed out, and wanted to get about the task at hand.

Do you might remember Yakov Smirnoff, a Russian comedian, who came to the United States in the late 1970s? He was not prepared for the incredible variety of instant products available in American grocery stores. In one of his comedy routines, he said, *'On my first shopping trip, I saw powdered milk – you just add water, and you get milk. Then, I saw powered orange juice – you just add water, and you get orange juice. And then I saw baby powder, and I thought to myself, "What a country America is!"'*[1]

But just as adding water to baby powder does not make babies, baptism doesn't make us into instant Christians. Our baptism is a faith starter for the decisions and struggles ahead, if we are going to follow Jesus. Jesus, who was always shockingly honest with his followers, was also honest about the price to be paid by those who decided to follow him. You would think that in those circumstances, he would soften the truth a bit to attract more followers – but not so with Jesus.

He continues, *'Do not think I have come to bring peace to the earth. No, I tell you, but rather division – family member against family member.'* When he spoke of this division in the family, ears must have perked up and tempers flared. Families have a high priority in our lives, but in Palestine, family relationships and parental approval were of primary importance for all of life's major decisions. Jesus was saying that although family relationships were extremely important, they were secondary to a relationship with God. Jesus was being honest; a decision for Jesus will separate us from the world, and that separation may well begin in our families.

Jesus was saying, *'As my followers you will need to make some hard decisions.'* There is a cost to being a Christian. Do we see it that way today? Do our lives reflect what we say we believe? Do we work as hard to fulfill the expectations we should have, as disciples of Jesus Christ, as we do to fulfill cultural expectations? Or have we bought into an acceptable, middle-class Christianity, a cultural Christianity with fewer demands, a comfortable Christianity rather than a costly Christianity? Yes, there is a cost to being a Christian, if we take it seriously.

Recently, I was reminded of that cost when my phone rang. It was a call from Tiffany, a woman who was staying at a domestic violence shelter. She had gotten my phone number from Bethlehem's answering machine. Tiffany needed $39.50 for a bus ticket to Joliet, where she had a reservation at another domestic violence shelter. Her abusive husband had found out where she was staying, so she had to leave for her own safety. Could I help her with the cost of a bus ticket? I went down my usual checklist of excuses: 1) Too Busy – I wasn't too busy; 2) Didn't Have Time – I did have the time; 3) No Money – I had just gotten $50 on a redeemed Christmas gift. Besides, Tiffany sounded solid and credible. Could this be Jesus in the disguise of an abused woman? My intuition gave me the go-ahead.

Since I didn't have any excuses, I asked where I could find her to give her the money. She identified a nearby Mc Donald's and we chose a time to meet. When I met her, the first thing I noticed was that she had nothing but the clothes on her back – no purse or sack or bag. She was also hungry, so that was our first priority. Then, I was ready to leave, to go home.

I casually asked if she knew where the bus station was. She didn't have a clue, but insisted she could walk there. I wasn't sure it was within walking distance, and the staff and customers of McDonalds didn't help. They gave us confusing directions to the Greyhound bus station. Some said, *'go east;'* others said, *'go west,'* that it was across the bridge. East won out because I knew a bus station in that part of town. Once at that station, we were given another address, and a helpful woman in the parking lot gave us directions. We found the road and a deserted-looking transit building; we weren't convinced we were at the right place until I saw a bus, and followed it. Tiffany checked out the terminal, and discovered we were in right place. That is the end of story – at least, the end of my part of story.

Hopefully, things work out for her at Joliet and she has a safer life. The cost to me wasn't much[2] – a little time and a little money – but I gained a new awareness of the vulnerability of domestic violence victims – of all the other Tiffanies – and I can't get that out of my mind.

In this Gospel, Jesus definitely has a message of tough love. First, he brings the fire of judgment on each of us. We cannot be confronted with Jesus and remain neutral – we are either for him or we are against him. Second, if we are for him, there is a price, because daily we must strive to have our beliefs, what we say, match our actions, what we do. So why is Jesus being so tough on us? He wants what is best for us. The bottom line is this: only total loyalty to God can satisfy the deepest longings of our souls and bring us satisfaction on earth and salvation in eternity.

Tough love is Good News when it comes from Jesus.

AMEN.

Scripture: Luke 12:49-56
August 14, 2016
Bethlehem Lutheran Church, Rockford, Ill.

HOLY CROSS DAY

CROSS ACTION[1]

During the years I have served as a pastor, I have come to realize that when someone says, *'there is someone here who needs to see a pastor,'* those are code words. They mean someone needs money, food or a referral. Several years ago, after worship, word came: *'There is a man waiting in the courtyard who needs to see a pastor.'* True to form, this man had a need, but a need I never would have suspected.

The gentlemen greeted me, and invited me to go with him to the front of the church. *'This is strange,'* I thought, *'I know the front of the church fairly well. What could he show me?'* He stopped in front of the cross and announced, *"I want you to take that down!"* *"Excuse me,"* I said, *"you want what?"* He replied, *"I want you to take that cross down."*

I could tell from the tone of his voice and from his facial expression that, for him, this was serious business. He proceeded to share his theology: *"You should take down the cross because it is a symbol of execution in the style of an ancient death row."* I could not argue. He continued, explaining the cross does not reflect the love of God, only the violence of men. His mission was to convince all churches to remove their crosses. He further claimed the cross in Jesus' day was comparable to the gun in our day. He concluded his argument with a question; he asked if we had considered displaying a gun in front of the church.

Again, he repeated, *"The cross needs to come down."* I shook my head and said, *"You do not know who you are dealing with. This is the Lutheran Church. We have a theology of the cross. The cross is central to what we confess; in the cross God meets us; through the cross God acted on behalf of all humanity."* I assured him, *"Don't waste your time with Lutherans – we are keeping the cross."* He shook my hand, jumped in his car, and sped off to try to convert the Presbyterians or Methodists to his way of thinking.

We are definitely keeping the cross. In fact, on Holy Cross Day, we celebrate the cross, rejoice in the cross, revere the cross, sing of the cross, and most of all, reflect on the actions of God through the cross.

Other religions have symbols of beauty and light – the six-pointed star, a crescent moon, or the lotus blossom. Ours is the cross – an instrument of torture and the cruelest of deaths. The cross is not as civilized as lethal injections, as sudden as hanging from the gallows, or as jolting as the electric chair. Death on the cross was slow and agonizing, done in the most humiliating way – in the public arena, where the victim was open to jeers and ridicule. Crucifixion was a horrific form of death. The victim, with arms outstretched, couldn't hold his head up, and often suffocated with his own head pressing down on his windpipe, or he drowned in his own blood as flies buzzed around and the sun beat down. The cross was a death to be feared.

And there Jesus hung, an innocent victim between two thieves. I am not saying he wasn't a radical – Jesus was radical when he hung out with sinners, lepers, women and tax collectors. I'm not saying Jesus didn't walk on the toes of the religious institution – he did. And he was 'in their faces' as he broke the rules and upset the tables in the temple. I'm not saying Jesus didn't make claims about his relationship to God; he did.

What I am saying is that he was crucified for seeing the world through God's eyes, for being in the world the way God wants all of us to be. He was crucified for having a God-shaped heart and for living a God-directed life.

Nails didn't keep Jesus on the cross. God's love – stretching from the foundation of the world until the end of time – kept Jesus on the cross. Love was concentrated in that moment – in that man. The vertical beams to heaven and the horizontal beams of humanity collided, and cross action occurred as the earth shook and the temple veil was torn. History was rewritten; time was reset.

Sin, death and the devil were defeated; hope was victorious. Don't misunderstand me: sin, death and the devil are still around, and they still have a word, but their word is not the final word. The cross without the empty tomb is incomplete. The God who brought resurrection out of the crucifixion brings hope where there is hopelessness. The cross is forever our symbol and our sign of the presence of God, of the promise of God, and of the power of God to act.

The cross is not historical; it is part of our experience now. So, when suffering is severe, when the only luck you have is no luck at all, when you think nothing else can go wrong, when it seems the only news is bad news, and the entire world is at war, the cross says, *'God is in the midst of it, reshaping, remolding, remaking to bring good out of bad.'*

The theology of the cross says our God is where you least expect a god to be. God's presence is hidden in weakness, silent in suffering, quiet in vulnerability, and present with the forsaken and dying. In the abyss of despair, God is there. In the depth of darkness, God is there. Our human attempts to find God are exposed, for in the cross God finds us. God finds us most profoundly at the point of our deepest reality – whatever that might be.

"A stumbling block to Jews and foolishness to Gentiles, but to those who are called – both Jew and Greek, Christ is the power of God – the wisdom of God."[3] Foolishness – yes, to the unbeliever it is foolishness. You can't measure the beauty of a rainbow with a caliper, nor can you weigh the grandeur of a mountain on a bathroom scale. Likewise, you cannot easily comprehend the divine power of God in the actions of the cross, but you can, with faith, live into an understanding of the presence and the power of God.

During the darkest days of the Civil War, President Abraham Lincoln was seen pacing back and forth in his office. An attaché asked, "Mr. President, you seem nervous tonight. What is it? Don't you think God is on our side?" President Lincoln stopped and responded, "I don't believe God takes sides. My question is – are we on God's side?" Are we on God's side? To be on God's side is to believe that in every situation – no matter how grim – seen or unseen, God is at work for good.

"Each and every cross can be a reminder of God's agenda for the world.[2] We are surrounded by crosses. My fear is that there are so many crosses used in frivolous ways in this world – in jewelry, on tattoos, on cake decorations – that we may become complacent, and the crosses will lose the powerful message they have for us. To me, the most powerful cross is the one used to express our faith – the cross placed on the forehead at the time of baptism, or on children as they come for a blessing at communion, or when you dip your finger in the font as you enter the church, or when the cross is traced on the forehead of a dying person. All these crosses declare that God is with us no matter what happens to us; they say we are claimed by God.

However, we also have crosses in our churches today. What do these crosses have in common? They are empty! The Spirit of the crucified one is set free in our midst to continue the cross action of God's wisdom and power in the world. The cross is empty – that is the Good News! And why is the cross empty? "Because God so loved the world that God gave his only Son that whosoever believes in him should not perish but have everlasting life."[4]

When you see the cross, ask why it is empty. And let the answer be: it is empty because the cross continues to turn sadness into celebrating, to change hopelessness into hope, and most importantly, to bring life out of death.

AMEN.

Scripture: Isaiah 50:4-9, James 3:1-12, and Mark 8:27-38
September 14, 2003
Lutheran Church of the Reformation, Washington, D.C

ALL SAINTS SUNDAY

SAINTLY SINNERS

On All Saints Sunday, we celebrate the communion of saints. Pope Boniface IV, in the seventh century, noted there were so many saints they filled all the days in the calendar; he was sure there would be more saints, so he designated one Sunday to honor all the potential saints – like us. All Saints Sunday is our day.

How many of you consider yourself a saint? Don't be shy, admit it. I must acknowledge there have been some saints who have acted strangely, and that might make us apprehensive about claiming the title. Do you remember St. Francis of Assisi, who was known to roll in the snow naked in order to control his lusty desires? (Those were the days before cold showers.) There was St. Maximilian, who was the first conscientious objector. He was drafted by the Roman army and refused to go, even though his father was a veteran. Of course, he was sentenced to death. At his beheading, he noticed the executioner was wearing shabby clothes, so he stripped himself of his new clothes and gave them to the executioner. Some strange saints have preceded us.

If you don't consider yourself a saint, then you must be a sinner. Right? Then All Saints Sunday is for you, too, because saints are sanctified sinners. We really don't need to get hung up on the labels, 'saints' and 'sinners,' because Jesus came to give us all a new identity, 'child of God.' Those of us splashed by the waters of baptism, marked by the cross of Christ, and sealed by the Holy Spirit belong to the family of God, and are on the fast track to sainthood. On All Saints Sunday, we celebrate the inheritance God has for all of us. We are no longer simply sinners, but are sanctified sinners, filled with the Holy Spirit. Granted, the battle isn't completely won yet; as Lutheran doctrine claims, we are both saint and sinner at the same time. I don't know about you, but on some days, I feel so saintly I can barely stand myself, and on other days, I am so sinful I hide my face.

A Native American story explains how I feel. A grandfather explained how he felt to his grandson: *'I feel as if I have two wolves fighting in my heart. One wolf is vengeful, angry, and mean. The other wolf is gentle, compassionate and loving'.* The grandson asked, *'Which wolf will win the battle of your heart?'* His grandfather answered, *'The one I feed.'*

The Beatitudes, the traditional text for All Saints Sunday, encourages us to feed the saint in our hearts by doing deeds that might seem insignificant, but have ultimate significance. Jesus taught using the beatitudes, because they were a common literary style – short, pithy, two-part affirmations that summed up common knowledge about the good life. They went something like this: *'Blessed are those with a good retirement plan, for their old age will be comfortable,'* or *'Blessed are those who exercise daily, for they shall live longer.'* The form of the beatitudes was common, but the content shocked the crowd. *'Blessed are the poor'* – which includes the hungry, weeping and despised. That was hard to hear because everyone wanted to avoid poverty – and Jesus said being poor was being blessed.

And that wasn't all! *'Woe to the rich, those who are full now and filled with laughter and love flattery.'* Ouch! Those hearing the Beatitudes for the first time could hardly believe their ears, because it was an absolute reversal of the way of the world. Jesus was saying: *'See the world the way God sees the world.'*

Jesus' message is this: God levels the playing field by standing the haves and have-nots on their heads. God re-orders life as we know it – the first will be last, winners will be declared losers, and insiders are outsiders. God's reversal turns pigs' ears into silk purses! Street people get the royal treatment! Soup lines lead to banquet halls! This confused the whole crowd, and confuses us still.

The Beatitudes are the end of the world as we know it, and the beginning of the world as God sees it. Sometimes we are on the down side in life, and sometimes we are on the upside. The most important thing to hear about the Beatitudes is that *they are not about us*. So, don't worry about which category – rich or poor, hungry or full – you are in. The Beatitudes are first and foremost about God. Once we understand they show us how God sees the world, then we can respond to the world as God sees it.

What Jesus is saying, by introducing the upside-down world of the Beatitudes, is supported by the Old Testament. Throughout the Old Testament, God spoke through the prophets in defense of the poor, widows, orphans, and those who could not fend for themselves. The Old Testament also makes reference to the poor as those who look to God to deliver them from all their troubles – so the disciples were called poor. Even as the Old Testament repeatedly defended the poor, the religious institution of Jesus' day created rules and regulations that kept those God favored on the outside. So, with the Beatitudes, Jesus was setting the record straight: this is how God sees the world and how God favors the people who depend on God.

How does God favor his people? God blesses them! Blessedness says we are valued and esteemed in God's sight. It says that out of obedience, we have chosen to be on God's side in this world, trusting God that all is not as it appears. There is more to life than meets the eye or can be measured by human standards. Therefore, even a life of deprivation can be a life of blessedness. Blessedness comes when we are right with God, and is not to be confused with happiness.

Sometimes we obsess about happiness and the pursuit of it. We all want happiness. But, happiness changes as we change and as the world changes. Blessedness comes when we believers trust our lives and our well-being to God for the long haul, beyond the horizon, rather than resting our hopes in the here and now of short-lived gains, with its pleasures and comforts in the present world. The saints we raise up today, those who have gone on to claim their baptismal promises, have stood firmly by faith in two worlds – the Kingdom of God, that we only glimpse in hints, and the Kingdom of the World that surrounds us. The saints that have gone before are living witnesses to the Beatitudes, because they have blessed us with their faithful living.

As we lift up the saints who have been part of our lives, we also lift up Southeast Ministry, which is a witness to the Beatitudes.[1] In 1990, Roger Truehart[2] and I began tutoring in a basement apartment at People's Cooperative on Elvan's Road, Southeast. At that time, programs for kids were few and far between, as were white people working in Ward 8. Roger was a very tall and serious Black man with a *'Don't mess with me'* attitude, and I was then, as I am now, a dumpy white woman. We made an interesting pair as we admitted to using gender, race, and class to the advantage of our programs as we tutored kids in public housing, introducing softball and flag football leagues.

One day after tutoring there was a very animated conversation between several fifth and sixth graders about my race. The kids were trying to decide if I was black or white. The lead argument was: *'no white woman would ever come over here to Southeast, so you can't be white.'* No matter what I said, or how I argued the point, they simply wouldn't accept the fact that I was Caucasian. It was too much for them to get their heads around, since they were saturated with preconceived ideas about what white people did and didn't do. One little girl (whose name I cannot recall, but whose face I can still see in my mind's eye) concluded that I was 'high-yeller,' meaning I had some African American ancestry. To her, the possibility that was 'high-yeller' resolved the dilemma of why a white lady would come to Southeast. James, the little boy, simply said, *'I win, you are black, that is that.'* He walked away – end of discussion – confident he had the final word.

That little encounter was truly a blessing to me, and still is. It reflected the Beatitudes; Roger and I had succeeded in setting the world those kids knew on its head, and in surprising ourselves, too. By the power of God, we don't have to accept the world the way it is. We, the servants of God, can turn the world upside down and usher in the Kingdom. We can see – and be part of the world – as God sees it, an upside-down, inside-out world, where racial boundaries are crossed with ease, differences are respected, and lives are shared.

The Beatitudes come to us and say there is more to life than meets the eye – sinners become saints and the dead are raised. And we earthbound creatures can claim heaven as our home. Thanks be to God!

AMEN.

Scripture: Luke 6:20-31
November 7, 2010
Lutheran Church of the Reformation, Washington, D.C.
20th Anniversary of Southeast Ministry

CHRIST THE KING SUNDAY

CRUCIFIED KING

Oxymorons are phrases with words that appear contradictory. They are words that simply don't seem to belong together such as 'downward mobility,' 'connoisseur of cheap wine,' 'cruel kindness,' 'angry love,' 'violent compassion' or 'short sermon for up-front Lutherans.' Do you get the idea? Christ the King Sunday is the last Sunday of the church year, when we attempt to grasp the entirety of Christ's life from the cradle to the cross, and from his conception to ascension. Much of it is filled with oxymorons.

The oxymoron most appropriate is Crucified King. Whoever heard of a crucified king? Kings are supposed to be powerful rulers. When Jesus hung on the cross, he appeared as powerless as the criminals who hung beside him. When he is hanging there, don't you want to say, 'Speak up, Jesus; say something; do something'? Instead, Jesus takes the bullying and absorbs the ridicule while the title, King of the Jews, hangs over his head.

Jesus doesn't say anything, but if you look closely, he uses his kingly powers in inconspicuous ways. Jesus forgives. Forgiveness was for God alone to give. Jesus is forgiving 'them' – those who, by dishonest and devious means, sentenced him; those who drove the nails through his hands and feet; those who were watching from the shadows, too scared to do anything. Jesus forgives all of them. He forgives all of us when we do things that perpetuate death and not life. The other kingly power Jesus exercised was that of granting salvation. Salvation was for God alone to give. Yet, Jesus granted the criminal salvation, and promised he would see Jesus in paradise.

His kingly powers were exercised so quietly, the crowds and soldiers didn't even notice. The crowds wanted Jesus to meet their expectations for an earthly king, one who would come down from the cross, rescued by a legion of angels. But, do you remember when Jesus was tempted in the wilderness? The devil offered him so much super-human power that he could mesmerize the people with his spectacular might, and people would immediately fall down believing.[1] Jesus refused that temptation then, and he refuses it from the cross.

Out of Jesus' mouth comes a thunderous silence as his coronation is taking place on the cross. Jesus, by his actions, is declaring, through pain and humiliation, that love is stronger than death, love is more powerful than the devil, and love is forgiveness in action. On the cross, unbeknownst to those around him, heaven and earth were united for *'in him all things are held together.'* The cross of Christ becomes the lynch pin of heaven and earth, the cosmic glue that gives purpose to our being, the reconciler of God and humanity. The cross is beautifully bad, where the worst of the world meets the best of God – and God wins.

Two angels were touring earth; one was older and more experienced, the other a young intern. In their travels, they stopped to spend the night at the mansion of a wealthy family. The family was inhospitable, and put the angels in a dark corner of the cold basement without supper. As the angels made their bed on the hard floor, the older angel noticed a hole in the wall and repaired it. When the younger angel asked why, the older angel replied, *'Things aren't always what* they *seem.'*

The next night, the pair came to rest at the home of a very poor, but hospitable farmer and his wife. After sharing what little food they had, the couple let the angels sleep in their bed with the best mattress and cozy quilts, so they could get a good night's rest. When the sun come up the next morning, the angels found the farmer and his wife in tears. Their only cow, whose milk was their sole source of income, lay dead in the field. The younger angel was furious at the older angel. *'Why did you let that happen? The rich family had everything, and treated us poorly, yet you helped them by repairing the hole in the wall. The poor family had little and was willing to share, and you let their cow die.'*

The older angel replied, *'Things aren't always what they seem. When we stayed in the basement of the mansion, I noticed there was gold stored in that hole in the wall. Since the owner was so obsessed with greed and unwilling to share, I sealed the wall so he couldn't find his gold. Then last night, as we slept in the farmer's bed, the angel of death came for his wife. I gave him the cow instead. Things aren't always what they seem.'*

No, things certainly are not what they seem. The incredible language of St. Paul's Letter to the Colossians waxes poetic about Christ being the image of the invisible God, where all the fullness of God was pleased to dwell. Through Christ, God reconciled to himself all things by *'making peace through the blood of the cross,'* in order for Jesus Christ to be the firstborn from the dead by the resurrection. Things are not always as they appear. Even as the King was crucified, there was a coronation on the cross.

We need Christ the King Sunday to remind us that Jesus of Nazareth, anointed by God as Jesus Christ, is more than just an approachable friend and constant companion. Jesus Christ is the Cosmic Christ, who is the glue that holds everything together. Christ was at the beginning – the Alpha – and he will be at the end – the Omega.[2] In the beginning when the Spirit of Christ moved across the face of the waters,[3] and a hundred thousand galaxies came into being – a plan arose in the heart of God to create a union with us, his people. That love became the throbbing pulse of all creation and shaped the life of Jesus, who walked the dusty roads of Nazareth and the crowded streets of Jerusalem, and sailed the Sea of Galilee. Through his teaching and preaching and healing, Jesus gave God a human face and a compassionate heart.

A quiet revolution was born that took history by the horns and changed life forever. Forever we would know our invisible God by his visible son; forever love would be defined by deeds, not creeds; and forever death would lose its sting. Jesus, who became God's anointed, made the loop from heaven above to earth; he came to bear Good News to everyone. And then, he returned to be seated at the right hand of God, leaving his Spirit, his Holy Spirit, here to continue the work he had begun.

What a God we have! What a gift we have been given in Jesus Christ! Jesus Christ is our constant companion, who lives with us and in us. He is also our Cosmic Christ, the Alpha and the Omega, holding all things together.

Alleluia! Alleluia! Our God reigns! Christ is the King!

AMEN.

Scripture: Luke 23:33-43; Colossians 1:11-20
November 24, 2013
Lake Preston/North Preston Lutheran Parish, Lake Preston, S.D.

NOTES

Introduction

1. Pilcher, Rosamunde. *The Shell Seekers*. St. Martin's Press, Dec. 15, 1987. Rosamunde Pilcher is a British writer who has published 28 novels in addition to a number of short stories. *The Shell Seekers* was a *New York Times* bestseller in 1988, and has been adapted into a play, a television mini-series, and a *Hallmark Hall of Fame* television film.

Pondering Heart

1. Sue Monk Kidd is a novelist and spiritual writer. Her first novel, *The Secret Life of Bees*, published by Viking Press in 2002, was on the New York Times list of bestsellers for more than two years. Other published works include: *When the Heart Waits: Spiritual Direction for Life's Sacred Questions* (HarperOne, 1990); *The Dance of the Dissident Daughter: a Woman's Journey from Christian Tradition to The Sacred Feminine* (HarperOne, 1966); *The Mermaid Chair* (Penguin Books, 2005); *Firstlight: The Early Inspirational Writings* (Penguin Books, 2007); *Traveling with Pomegranates: A Mother and Daughter Journey to the Sacred Places of Greek, Turkey and France* (with Ann Kidd Taylor, Penguin Books, 2009); and *The Invention of Wings* (Penguin Books, 2014).

2. Meister Eckhardt (1260-1328?) is a 14th Century Christian mystic and Dominican monk said, "If the only prayer you ever say in your life is thank you, it will be enough." Eckhardt fell into obscurity following his death in 1328, but was rediscovered in the 19th Century. Contemporary theologians such as Matthew Fox have drawn upon his work in their own writings.

Christmas Tonight!

1. Brooks, Phillips. "Everywhere, Everywhere Christmas To-Night: A Christmas Carol." *Christmas Songs and Easter Carols,* ed. Phillips Brooks, E.P. Dutton & Company, 1903.

2. Dr. Seuss. *How the Grinch Stole Christmas!* Random House Books for Young Readers, Oct. 12, 1957.

Baptismal Blessings

1. The words spoken at a child's baptism are taken from "The ELCA Service of Holy Baptism" found in the *Lutheran Book of Worship*, published by Augsburg Fortress. The most recent edition was published in October 2006.

Why Was I Born?

1. Time Magazine. *Special Mind and Body Issue: The Secret of Happiness.* Time, Inc., Jan. 17, 2005.

2. Paul Tillich (1886-1965) was a Lutheran theologian and existentialist philosopher, who moved to the United States in 1933 after losing his position at the University of Frankfurt when his lectures brought him into conflict with the Nazi movement in Germany. Like fellow German, Dietrich Bonhoeffer, and German-educated Karl Barth, he is considered one of the leading theologians of the 20th Century. His works include: *The Courage to Be* (Yale University Press, 1952); *Dynamics of Faith* (Harper & Row, 1957); *Theology and Culture* (Oxford University Press, 1959); and *Morality and Beyond* (Harper & Row, 1963).

3. King, Martin Luther, Jr. "A Christmas Sermon for Peace," Dec. 24, 1967. King (1929-1968), Baptist minister and Nobel Peace Prize recipient, is known for being a strong leader in the civil rights movement in the United States in the 1950s and 1960s. His famous "I Have a Dream" speech, delivered in the 1963 March on Washington, was just one of the numerous ways he worked to combat racial inequity through non-violence. He was awarded the Presidential Medal of Freedom and the Congressional Gold Medal posthumously. In 1986, a federal holiday was established to honor his legacy.

4. When Pastor McNeill preached this sermon, she included very specific examples:

"We are all shocked and saddened by the loss of over 162,000 lives in the Asian tsunami. Yet, nearly 40,000 lives are lost on a daily basis worldwide from starvation and its complications. Closer to home, in the metro area of this city of great wealth and influence, over 20,000 people are homeless – 40% of them are families. Or even closer still – the number of food bags given out by Church of the Reformation has tripled in the last two years... why the increase? What is happening in our community that leaves so many people hungry? There is much justice work to do."

Stop Pretending: Ash Wednesday Meditation
  1. Psalm 51:17
  2. Psalm 145:8

Resurrection Hope
  1. Cf. Romans 8:11

Politics of Compassion
  1. Cf. Leviticus 19:2, 1 Peter 1:16
  2. Cf. 1 Kings 17:17-24

Prayer Beyond All Prayers
  1. American theologian Reinhold Niebuhr is credited with writing the original Serenity Prayer: "God grant me the serenity to accept the things I cannot change, the courage to change the things I can, and the wisdom to know the difference." It has become the cornerstone of 12-Step programs such as that used by Alcoholics Anonymous and Narcotics Anonymous. The author of the revised version is unknown.
  2. Cf. Romans 8:26

The Good News of Tough Love
  1. Yakov Smirnoff is a Russian-born entertainer, who has been in movies with some of America's leading actors, including *"Moscow on the Hudson"* with Robin Williams and *"The Money Pit"* with Tom Hanks. Prior to the fall of the Soviet Union, he did stand-up comedy, mocking both communism and consumerism. For more information, see his website at: www.yakov.com.
  2. Pastor McNeill indicates the cost to her "wasn't much," but the cost would have been greater than her words suggest. By this time, the Idiopathic Pulmonary Fibrosis had advanced to the point that she required oxygen 24/7 and tired easily. Assisting Tiffany would have taken a great person toll, but she did not see it this way. Like St. Paul, who wrote in his letter to the Philippians, "I have suffered the loss of all things, and count them but rubbish so that I may gain Christ" (3:8), Pastor McNeill would have considered her suffering to be part of her journey with Christ.

Cross Action

1. The nave of the Lutheran Church of the Reformation is in the Art Deco style, richly ornamented with religious symbols. For more information about the church, please see *"The Architecture and Symbolism of the Lutheran Church of the Reformation"* by Elizabeth Johns (published in 1985), available online through the Art Deco Society of Washington (www.adsw.org).

During the sermon, Pastor McNeill left the pulpit and made reference to specific church features. Because the reader will not have those visual references, that portion of the sermon was edited for clarity. However, that passage is included in full in the Notes so that anyone who visits the church or worships there can appreciate how beautifully Pastor McNeill wove together the building and Lutheran theology of the cross. About this sermon, Pastor McNeill said, "The congregation applauded. It was an exhilarating and solidifying experience for the congregation, and is still referred to as the 'cross sermon.'"

2. When Pastor McNeill preached this sermon, she left the pulpit at this point. This is what she said, referring to features in the nave of the church:

"Each and every cross can be a reminder of God's agenda for the world. Look around you – go ahead and look. You are surrounded by crosses, hundreds of crosses. In this lovely art work of so many crosses, sermons are preached to us. My fear is that there are so many crosses used in frivolous ways in this world – in jewelry, on tattoos, on cake decorations – that we may become complacent, and the crosses will lose the powerful message they have for us. To me, the most powerful cross is the one used to express our faith – the cross placed on the forehead at the time of baptism, or on children as they come for a blessing at communion, or when you dip your finger in the font as you enter the church, or when the cross is traced on the forehead of a dying person. All these crosses declare that God is with us no matter what happens to us; they say we are claimed by God.

"Let's look closely at the crosses on our ceiling: the ones in the center are called the king post; on each cross is a shield from the disciples. Then, there are east and west beam supports, starting with the Latin cross on which Jesus was crucified, then a cross formed like a four-pointed star, then the cross of the Crusades, an interwoven cross, a cross quadrant, a beautiful decorative cross with each beam ending in three petals, and the next one is nearly the same, but the petals represent the Holy Trinity, and finally the cross of the catacombs. Down the west beams are the Latin cross, then a series of decorative crosses like the others, and the fifth one is the Cross Crosslet to represent the four corners of the earth; the sixth is the Greek cross that a perfect circle can enclose; then St. Andrew's cross, on which he died, and the Maltese cross, which spearheads join in the center.

"What do all these crosses have in common? They are empty! The Spirit of the crucified one is set free in our midst to continue the cross action of God's wisdom and power in the world. The cross is empty – that is the Good News! And why is the cross empty? Because God so loved the world that God gave his only Son that whosoever believes in him should not perish but have everlasting life."

    3. 1 Corinthians 1:23-24

    4. John 3:16

Saintly Sinners

    1. This sermon was preached on the 20th Anniversary of the Southeast Ministry, a social justice ministry in Washington, D.C., which helps welfare mothers and ex-offenders achieve self-sufficiency through job-readiness programs and other educational programs. The sermon has been edited for clarity, but here is that portion of the sermons as it was preached:

    "As we lift up the saints who have been part of our lives, we also lift up Southeast Ministry on its 20th Anniversary – it, too, is a witness to the Beatitudes. Today is a day overflowing with emotion; the last 20 years have had many ups and downs, as do most journeys in life that are worth taking. Southeast Ministry has been a journey of obedience for it was the call of the Holy Spirit that gave birth to this social-justice ministry in Ward 8; and it was through the empowerment of the Holy Spirit that it has continued. Southeast Ministry has been a journey of mutual blessings for both the Church of the Reformation and Southeast Ministry, introducing new realities into each other's worlds, stretching understanding and compassion in both directions. Southeast Ministry has been a journey with abundant blessings as well as challenges as we lived out the belief that God is a God of justice; therefore, it is our obligation, as disciples, to actively pursue justice for all.

    "In 1990, Roger Truehart and I began tutoring in a basement apartment at People's Cooperative on Elvan's Road, Southeast. At that time, programs for kids were few and far between as were white people working in Ward 8. Roger was a very tall and serious Black man with a *'Don't mess with me'* attitude, and I was then, as I am now, a dumpy white woman. We made an interesting pair as we admitted to using gender, race, and class to the advantage of our programs as we tutored kids in public housing, introducing softball and flag football leagues.

"One day after tutoring there was a very animated conversation between several fifth and sixth graders about my race. Do I look anything but white? Evidently not to the kids, because they were trying to decide if I was black or white. The lead argument was: *'no white woman would ever come over here to Southeast, so you can't be white.'* No matter what I said, or how I argued the point – after all just look at my hair, my nose, my skin – they simply wouldn't accept the fact that I was Caucasian. It was too much for them to get their heads around, since they were saturated with preconceived ideas about what white people did and didn't do. One little girl (whose name I cannot recall, but whose face I can still see in my mind's eye) concluded that I was 'high-yeller,' meaning I had some African American ancestry. To her, the possibility that was 'high-yeller' resolved the dilemma of why a white lady would come to Southeast. James, the little boy, simply said, *'I win, you are black, that is that.'* He walked away – end of discussion – confident he had the final word."

2. Roger Truehart was born on July 5, 1947, and died on April 24, 2004. Funeral services were held at the Lutheran Church of the Reformation on May 12, 2004. Little information about him is available online. However, he is described as an activist intellectual in "Preaching a Gospel of Personal Responsibility" by Stephen Goode (*Insight on the News*, Vol. 17, No. 17, May 7, 2001). In speaking of the work at Southeast in that interview, he said, "It is a team concept in which each of us brings our own experience to apply to each situation. Normally we deal with 18-year-olds and older. A young lady or a guy comes to us and we sit down and have this dialogue. We have this face-to-face experience so that we can assess whatever problems there are. It's important that we don't go with what's in our face, meaning we work to get past stereotypes." Relating to each person as an individual rather than as a stereotype is part of the upside-down world of the Beatitudes Pastor McNeill explores in this sermon.

Crucified King
1. Cf. Luke 4:5-8
2. Cf. Revelations 22:13
3. Cf. Genesis 1:2

Photograph for the Lake Preston Times by Mary Gales Askren ©

WANDA MCNEILL: BIOGRAPHICAL SKETCH

Rev. Wanda McNeill has lived a life of service, a life infused with gospel values, one which enabled her to teach by example what it means to live the gospel in our world. She was born in Sioux City, Iowa, and grew up on a farm east of Sioux City. Her first vocation was that of a registered nurse. She served first as a Vista volunteer, and later as a public health nurse, in North Carolina, where she also founded the Yancey County Hospice Agency. During her time there, she and her husband Frank McNeill were also the foster parents for 12 children.

Her second vocation was as an ordained minister with the Evangelical Lutheran Church of America. She graduated from Lutheran Theological Seminary in Gettysburg, Penn., in 1988 and was ordained in 1989. Later, in 2005, she also earned a Doctorate of Ministry from Lutheran Theological Seminary in Gettysburg. Pastor McNeill served as the assistant pastor, associate pastor and pastor of the Lutheran Church of the Reformation in Washington, D.C., from

1990 to 2007, when she stepped down to accept another call. During that time, she also co-founded a non-profit social justice ministry to help ex-offenders and welfare mothers achieve self-sufficiency through job-readiness programs. The website for the Southeast Ministry describes its work (and Pastor McNeill's legacy) in this way: "SEM's programs have changed countless lives. Through AMEN (Anacostia Mentoring and Employment Network), people learn real-world job skills and are assisted with job placement in diverse fields. For these men and women, learning to be an employee can be a new experience, and the staff of SEM puts them on the right path."

Pastor McNeill returned to her rural roots in 2007 when she moved to South Dakota to pastor the Lake Preston and North Preston Lutheran churches. She served there until retiring in 2014, a year after being diagnosed with Idiopathic Pulmonary Fibrosis. Following her retirement, she served as interim pastor at Bethlehem Lutheran Church in Rockford, Ill., until August 2016. At that time, feeling she still had more to offer, she gleaned from her sermons those included in this book so that she can continue to share what she has learned and lived.

Mary Gales Askren
Christmas 2016

38886391R00054

Made in the USA
Middletown, DE
29 December 2016